THE HANDBOOK
ON
PLUMERIA CULTURE

by

Richard M. and Mary Helen Eggenberger

Fourth Edition

Revised and Expanded

Plumeria obtusa "Singapore"

(clockwise from noon) **Grove Farm, Slaughter Pink, Japanese Lantern, Dwarf Deciduous, Mela Matson, Scott Pratt, Mary Moragne, Gold, Dean Conklin,** (center) **Penang Peach.**

Richard & Mary Helen Eggenberger

THE·HANDBOOK·ON
PLUMERIA
CULTURE

*Flowers are the moment's representation
of things that are in themselves eternal.*

Sri Aurobindo

FOURTH EDITION
REVISED AND EXPANDED

Fourth Edition
Revised and Expanded

Published by
GOLDEN BRIDGE PUBLICATIONS
A division of Auromère Inc.
2621 W. Hwy 12
Lodi, CA 95242
1-800-735-4691
www.plumeriasandoleanders.com
Fourth Edition 2005

Unless otherwise noted, all
Photographs and Illustrations
by
Richard and Mary Helen Eggenberger

Line drawings by Mary Helen Eggenberger

Front Cover
Plastic Pink
Back Cover
The Artistic Lei Makers of Hawaii

Library of Congress Catalog Number
88-092641
ISBN 0-9643224-0-4

DEDICATION

To our colleagues and friends,
fellow travellers and seekers;
To all who aspire for a
world of peace and harmony
and for whom the language of the flowers
and their spiritual message
is the uplifting hand of beauty
guiding us on the path
to realization.

PREFACE TO THE FOURTH EDITION

Since the publication of the third edition of <u>The Handbook on Plumeria Culture</u>, we've seen a meteoric rise in the popularity of plumerias. Plumerias are now available at specialty nurseries in many parts of the country and even more sources are found through mail order catalogs.

The year 2000 has arrived, the dawn of a new millennium, one of unprecedented challenge and possibility. We wish to take this opportunity to thank all of our plumeria friends who have kept in touch these many years, telling us of their wonderful experiences with plumerias and oleanders (our second book). We remember them with deep affection. Among those who have done the most to advance the cause of plumerias and to whom we express our gratitude are Emerson and Nancy Willis of La Porte, Texas, who have made innumerable journeys in their "plumeriamobile" named "Nan and the Plumeria Man", collecting and distributing plumerias throughout the country. Their mobile home should also be listed in the <u>Guiness Book of World Records</u> since it displays the world's largest photo of a plumeria! Our thanks also to our dedicated friends, Paul Tomaso and Harry Leuzinger who carried on the work of The Plumeria People for many years, and to Glenn and Yvonne Stokes who have amassed the most extensive collection of plumerias in the U.S. and offer them through their beautiful mail order catalog. Lastly, a special thanks to all the wonderful members of The Plumeria Society of America for their warm friendship spanning nearly twenty years. Their enthusiasm has broadened considerably the gardening public's appreciation for the beauty and magnificence of plumerias.

We are pleased to mention that a number of gardeners have taken up tip grafting to preserve and increase the rarest varieties in a simple and effective way. Here's how it is done. Take a growing tip from a desired scion just before or as it is beginning to leaf out. Cut a "V" shaped wedge at the bottom and insert into a "V" cut in the desired stock. People who use this simple wedge graft often insert a pin or needle through stock and scion to hold the scion in place. You may also use a standard "whip and tongue" graft described in any book on grafting and the scion will hold in place. In either case, you can then wrap with grafting tape or electrical tape or even duct tape. As always, the most important thing is to match the cambium of stock and scion. A new technique for rooting cuttings is girdling a stem chosen for a cutting while still attached to the mother plant by cutting away a ring of cambium around it. Many growers have found that by allowing the girdled area to harden on the plant the cutting will root more easily than one that has been cut off and then allowed to harden off for a few days. This technique is useful for some of the difficult-to-root cultivars. Lastly, a suggestion for overwintering from Harry Leuzinger — keep newly planted plumerias in pots for the first year and allow them to put on as much root growth as possible in a sunny area away from freezing temperatures, then store them in the second year according to the techniques listed in our "Overwintering" chapter.

CONTENTS

FORWARD
WITH ACKNOWLEDGEMENTS

For many the love of plumerias has blossomed with a visit to a tropical climate, especially Hawaii or the Caribbean. A first glance at these extraordinary tropical trees and shrubs, bedecked with hundreds of scented blooms in a rainbow of colors, has inspired thousands to attempt to transplant this magical, exotic experience to the home garden. Who would not wish to have the beauty and fragrance of Frangipani flowers for arrangements, to wear in the hair or to admire in the landscape even as they fall and carpet the earth.

Thus, for many, begins a lifelong fascination and ambition, not merely to propagate and grow plumerias, often in climates that are anything but tropical, but to bring them into bloom so that we may delight in their many enchanting fragrances, their subtle or intense colors and color combinations and their surprising range of size and shape. To achieve this, we need to know all about caring for them; how to protect plants during cold weather (for plumerias are indeed true tropicals and cannot tolerate a freeze); what fertilizers are most beneficial; which varieties are the most beautiful, fragrant, most floriferous, and so forth.

Our love of plumerias began at the other end of the earth, in Auroville, India. Auroville is an international township involving participation by people from all parts of the world, supported by public and private contributions and endorsed by three resolutions of UNESCO. Inaugurated on February 28, 1968, Auroville is located on the east coast of India, a few miles north of the former French province of Pondicherry and about 100 miles south of the major city of Madras, on the Bay of Bengal. Auroville is a dream in the process of becoming a reality, a testing ground where the Ideal of Human Unity may be nurtured and allowed to grow; a model city where the higher ideals of mankind can find expression and fulfillment.

In 1969 I was invited to create twelve gardens to surround the Matrimandir, the spiritual and geographical center of the city. Each of the Matrimandir Gardens symbolizes a higher attribute of life with specially selected plants and flowers. The plumeria was chosen to represent the Garden of Perfection. From humble beginnings on a few acres of parched, overgrazed and severely eroded land with little or no water supply, the Matrimandir Gardens grew into a botanical paradise of tropical color and fragrance with pools of lotus and waterlilies, over 5000 specie and hybrid orchids, numerous hibiscus and more than 2000 other tropical plants collected from all parts of India and sent to us through the courtesy of botanical gardens throughout the world. We created 300 of our own hibiscus hybrids and had plants that produced as many as 600 flowers a day! The seasons were filled with the glory of tropical trees, the resplendence of cassias in bloom, the brilliance of the Flamboyant, the captivating fragrance of peltaphorum, the splendor of massive bouquets of bougainvilleas (often in such full bloom that not a leaf was visible), the luxuriant spikes of Crape myrtles, and fields and fields of plumerias!

From 1970 to 1981, Mary Helen and I and several of our colleagues travelled extensively to study and collect plumeria species and hybrids from many areas of the world. We journeyed throughout India, visiting major botanic gardens, agricultural and horticultural experiment stations, horticultural societies and private gardens. On a plant collecting expedition in Southeast Asia, we visited the Singapore Botanic Garden and were given many named varieties of plumerias through the generosity of the director of the Gardens. In fact, everywhere we travelled and searched for new varieties, colors, forms and fragrances of plumerias, we were welcomed. From parks and homes, institutes and temples, people graciously donated cuttings. We also collected plants from the wild and grew hundreds of seedlings from superior parent plants.

In all, we amassed more than 140 different cultivars, at least five distinct species and more than 300 seedlings for evaluation and selection and, on any day of the year, we had a minimum of 35-40 different plumerias in bloom! During this time we corresponded with numerous botanists and horticulturists, developed seed exchange programs with more than 80 botanic gardens in 30 nations and were assisted by men and women of goodwill throughout the world.

Our special thanks go to the many friends who helped us realize our goals. A few we have met only through correspondence, some we have had the good fortune to visit often and form lifelong friendships.

First of all, our special thanks to Elizabeth Thornton, author of The Exotic Plumeria, and her husband Jim, for their generosity and encouragement and the many years of sharing experiences with plumerias. Through Elizabeth's efforts the Plumeria Society of America was founded. Her love and enthusiasm in promoting public awareness of plumerias is widely acknowledged and appreciated, as is her research in all areas of plumeria culture.

To Dr. James L. Brewbaker of the University of Hawaii for his assistance in helping us build the plumeria collection at the Matrimandir Gardens through the introduction of many Hawaiian hybrids.

To Dr. Richard A. Criley of the University of Hawaii for all his help during the past nine years; for sending us seeds of outstanding cultivars from his collection at the University; for his sharing of fundamental research and his prompt replies to our corespondence.

To Keith Woolliams and his staff at Waimea Arboretum and Botanical Gardens for their generosity in exchanging plant materials, their readiness to share information and ideas, and for their contribution of wild-collected species from the Dominican Republic which grow luxuriantly at the Matrimandir Gardens today.

To the Directors of all the botanical gardens who have given us plumeria seeds and plants and have graciously assisted us in research; especially to the Director of the

Kebun Raya Botanical Garden in Bogor, Indonesia, one of the finest gardens in Asia; to Mr. Hardial Singh of the Singapore Botanic Garden for giving us cuttings of their entire plumeria collection; to the Directors of the Lal-Bagh Gardens in Bangalore, India, and the Calcutta Botanic Gardens for sharing their collections with us.

To Mrs. Dorothy Fernando, our gracious hostess during our collecting trips in Sri Lanka and whose watercolors of plumerias are the finest we have seen; to a neighbor of Mrs. Fernando, the noted author, Arthur C. Clarke, who shared cuttings of his cultivars with us.

Special thanks to all our friends in India who share our love for plumerias (and all plants!); especially to Yagna Sastri of the Theosophical Society, Madras; Dr. T.A. Ramakrishnan of Trivandrum; Mr. R. Haresh of Madurai for his interest in collecting plumerias and other beautiful plants from all areas of the world and his willingness to share with fellow collectors; and to Sri Parichand, elder brother and mentor, who has tended the gardens of the Sri Aurobindo Ashram in Pondicherry for more years than we can recall and whose love of light blossoms in him and in his flowers.

Our thanks also to some wonderful friends in Houston; to Nancy Ames and Danny Ward, for years of friendship and a shared love of plumerias that we mutually agree have chosen us and not the reverse, and the special warmth of an inner relationship that transcends time and the passing of years; to Lydia Hilliard for her kindness and generosity during her term as President of the Plumeria Society of America and beyond, especially in sharing the wealth of her garden; to all the members of the Plumeria Society of America for their love of plumerias and their friendship, their kindness to me during my terms as Vice-President and President, and to some very special friends in the Society, Betty Andrews, Dave Emison, and Abe and Mary Schonier, among others, whose love and interest in growing plumerias runs deep and true.

To the many garden writers and editors all over the world who have encouraged gardeners to grow plumerias through articles and radio programs; especially to Elvin McDonald, a true friend and plantsman, who has championed the plumeria in his numerous syndicated articles in the U.S.

To friends in Hawaii who have contributed to the growing appreciation of plumerias; to Jim Little who has studied the culture of plumerias for years and has contributed his own hybrids to the wealth of cultivars we enjoy today; to Mrs. Sam Cooke (Mary Moragne), daughter of the late Bill Moragne, for sharing with us a large body of information on her father's seminal work in hybridization. To those whom we have not met, or visited only briefly, but who have been instrumental in furthering the appreciation and preservation of plumerias; Donald Angus, whose generosity to the University of Hawaii has enabled numerous research projects to be undertaken, and who collected and donated many of the finest cultivars to the University of Hawaii; authors Donald P. Watson, James T. Chinn, Horace F. Clay and others who have contributed to our understanding of plumerias; and lastly, to the hundreds of gardeners around the world who write us regularly of their experiences with plumerias and other fascinating and rewarding exotic plants.

Plastic Pink

Samoan Fluff

Katie Moragne

Pure Gold

Jean Moragne

Nebel's Rainbow

Candy Stripe

Lei Rainbow

INTRODUCTION

ON THE SIGNIFICANCE OF FLOWERS

The study of plants and flowers is twofold; a gradual and progressive inner awakening to their spiritual nature and their messages, and the day to day physical work that teaches us through beauty, the discipline of understanding their needs and assisting them in manifesting their ultimate perfection. As we turn more and more within, we may also awaken to our own inner nature and allow it to flower. A scientific discipline is essential in working with physical matter, as is the aspiration to go deeper within and contact the force behind the form and finally, to truly love and eventually enter into a pyschic contact with the splendor of this divine creation.

We hear daily of wondrous experiences with plants. We all know someone with a "green thumb" who, in answer to how they grow plants of unearthly beauty would simply say that they talk to their plants and love them. Or perhaps we have read the research of authors such as Peter Tompkins and Christopher Bird whose book, The Secret Life of Plants, is ". . . a fascinating account of the physical, emotional and spiritual relations between plants and man." Then, too, there are the the organic gardeners, the true children of the soil, whose work vibrates with an appreciation for the unity of all life as exemplified in the gardens of Findhorn and Auroville.

In all the literature we have found on the significance and symbolism of flowers, none speaks with the force of Flowers and Their Messages, a collection and description of the significances of hundreds of flowers as perceived by The Mother of the Sri Aurobindo Ashram and founder of Auroville in India. It is a lifelong work that guides us into the inner world of nature to reveal a luminous creation of which we are only on the threshold. We quote some words of The Mother on love and aspiration in plants:

> The movement of love is not limited to human beings and it is perhaps less distorted in worlds other than the human world. Look at the flowers and trees. When the sun sets and all becomes silent, sit down for a moment and put yourself into communion with Nature. You will feel, rising from the earth, from below the roots of the trees and mounting upward and coursing through their fibres, up to the highest outstretching branches, the aspiration of an intense love and longing — a longing for something that brings light and gives happiness, for the light that is gone

and they wish to have back again. There is a yearning so pure and intense that if you can feel the movement in the trees, your own being too will go up in an ardent prayer for the peace and light and love that are unmanifested here.

Have you ever watched a forest with all its countless trees and plants struggling to catch the light — twisting and trying in a hundred ways to be in the sun? That is precisely the feeling of aspiration in the physical — the urge, the movement, the push towards the light. Plants have more of it in their physical being than man. Their whole life is a worship of light. Light is of course the material symbol of the Divine, and the sun represents, under material conditions, the supreme Consciousness. The plants feel it quite distinctly in their own simple, blind way. Their aspiration is intense if you know how to become aware of it.

As soon as there is organic life, the vital element is there, and it is this vital element that gives to flowers the sense of beauty. It is not perhaps individualised in the sense we understand it, but it is a sense of the species and the species always tries to realise it. I have noticed a first elementary psychic vibration in plant life, and truly the blossoming of a flower is the first sign of the psychic presence. The psychic individualises itself only in man, but it existed before him; only it is not the same kind of individualisation, it is more fluid and manifests as force or as consciousness rather than as individuality. Take the rose, for example, its great perfection of form, colour and smell expresses an aspiration and is a psychic gift. Look at a rose opening in the morning with the first contact of the sun — it is a magnificent self-giving aspiration!

Since flowers are the manifestation of the psychic in the vegetal kingdom, love of flowers would mean that one is drawn by the psychic vibration and consequently by the psychic in one's own self. When you are receptive to the psychic vibration, that puts you in a more intimate contact with the psychic in your own self. Perhaps the beauty of flowers too is a means used by Nature to awaken in human beings the attraction for the psychic.

The significance given to the plumeria by The Mother is 'Psychological Perfection'. She has written, "There is not one psychological perfection but five, like the five petals of this flower. We have said they are: sincerity, faith, devotion, aspiration and surrender."

With this beginning, we enter into a world of loveliness and fascination, the world of the plumeria, the Frangipani or Lei flower; to discover the keys to its culture and flowering, to be uplifted by its beauty.

PLUMERIAS AND THE APOCYNACEAE FAMILY

The plumeria has truly become the flower of the decade. As people travel more and visit tropical areas of the world, they cannot help but be enchanted by the beauty of this unique and exotic plant. The plumeria is a member of the Apocynaceae, a family which includes many horticultural treasures. Among these are the Oleanders and Periwinkles, Allamandas and Mandevillas, the Star Jasmine (*Trachelospermum*) and others too numerous to mention. Many are delightfully scented as well, though none with the many fragrances of the plumeria. The name, Apocynaceae, was given by A.L. de Jussieu in 1789. There are 200 genera and at least 2000 species in this Dogbane family which is widespread in tropical and sub-tropical regions and is characterized by almost all of its members having a milky white latex, entire leaves, the five lobes of the corolla convoluted and twisted in the bud, and seeds with a large straight embryo, often comose.

To many the plumeria still remains a mysterious exotic with a strange sounding name. Unlike roses, bulbs, orchids, cacti and other plant groups, very little has been written on its history or culture. We have been growing plumerias for more than twenty years, both here in the U.S. and in the tropics, and have seen the popularity of the plumeria increase dramatically in recent years. For most plumeria enthusiasts who have seen large trees in full bloom in the tropics without any care whatsoever, the problem in temperate and sub-tropical areas is not so much in growing the plant as getting it to flower and then preserving it over long, cold winters.

To help make growing plumerias as easy and successful as possible for everyone, we have written this second, expanded edition of our <u>Handbook on Plumeria Culture</u>, combining our experiences with those of plumeria growers throughout the world who have shared with us the colorful and fragrant rewards of their labors.

FAMILY MEMBERS
(see photos on pages 62 and 63)

The following plants are all in the same family as plumerias and make delightful and colorful companions.

Adenium obesum (Desert Rose) — This genus contains about four species native to tropical Africa, the most well-known being the Desert Rose. One of the true stars of the Apocynaceae family, this slow growing plant is execellent for bonsai culture and even when young will produce magnificent, rich rose-red blooms set against dark green leaves. Adenium obesum is very drought resistant and requires minumum watering since moisture is stored in its swollen trunk.

Allamanda — A family of approximately 12 species, all native to tropical America. The showy flowers range from yellow to purple and are borne in profusion over a long blooming season. Many new cultivars in striking shades of cream and rose-purple have been introduced in the past few years. Recent intoductions have also included exceptionally dwarf forms that bear full-sized blooms! Plants range from the new dwarf hybrids, erect small shrubs and modest-sized clambering shrubs in the cultivated forms to great lianas in native habitats. Most allamandas perform best in full sun but will bloom in conditions where they receive sun for at least a half day.

Allamanda carthartica — Probably the best known of the allamandas in American gardens. The form pictured here is a A. cathartica var. 'Hendersonii', commonly known as 'Brown Bud' Allamanda. Flowers are very large, to 5 inches, and bloom continually from spring to fall.

Allamanda cathartica 'Cherries Jubilee' (aka 'Chocolate Cherry') — The large flowers, (up to 4 inches in diameter), produced by this new cultivar are a delightful mixture of rose and lavender tones.

Allamanda Williamsii var. 'Stansill's Double' — This first fully double cultivar produces strikingly handsome blooms over many months. It is an excellent container plant and even makes a great ground cover in warm areas.

Carissa — A genus with approximately 35 species of small evergreen shrubs and trees, mostly with spines. Native to the Old World Tropics, the most popular species make handsome hedges or ground covers and produce an abundance of fragrant white to pinkish flowers. Some species produce edible pink fruits that make an excellent jam. Pictured is one of the compact forms of **Carissa grandiflora 'Compacta'**, a low growing ground cover or small hedge plant that flowers freely throughout spring and summer.

Catharanthus — About five species of erect annual or perennial herbs native to the Old World tropics. The most popular form is **Catharanthus roseus (Madagascar Periwinkle; Old Maid)**, native from India to Madagascar. In the past 5 to 10 years plant breeders have created some of the most beautiful hybrids imaginable, with much larger flowers, greater disease resistance, more compact forms and a wealth of new colors.

Mandevilla — All Mandevillas are native to tropical America, especially Argentina, Bolivia, and Brazil. This large genus comprises about 100 species, usually vines and scandent shrubs.

Mandevilla x amabilis 'Alice du Pont' — A regal, magnificent, small and floriferous vine with large, bright pink flowers set against dark green leaves. An excellent plant for containers.

Mandevilla boliviensis 'White Dipladenia' — A species recently introduced to the U.S. in 1993 that flowers even in small 4 inch pots. It is a small vine easily grown in containers and producing bloom from early spring into fall.

Nerium oleander — **(Common Oleander; Rose Bay)** — Native from the Mediterranean region to Japan, this is a large and colorful genus with hundreds of cultivars ranging from white to cream, pink, red, salmon, yellow, apricot, lilac, purple, carmine, copper and even orange! There are basically three flower types; single, semi-double (hose in hose), and fully double with many possessed of a sweet frangrance. Forms with variegated leaves are not uncommon as well as new cultivars with richly variegated flowers.

Nerium oleander 'Mrs. George Roeding' — A very lovely oleander with large semi-double, sweetly fragrant flowers in soft pastel shades of salmon, orange and cream. Intermediate in height.

Nerium oleander 'Martha Hanna Hensley' — One of the newest and most beautiful cultivars of the '90's, with delicate pink and white variegated flowers borne in large tight clusters and emitting a light delicate fragrance. Plants bloom when very young, flower over many months and can easily be grown in containers.

Nerium oleander 'Mathilde Ferrier' — Soft yellow, fully double flowers adorn this plant which is freeze tolerant in Zone 9. The variety is beautiful when grown as a shrub and makes an excellent hedge or is equally striking pruned as a small multi-branched tree.

Tabernaemontana — A genus of more that 110 species grown primarily for their decorative blooms, usually white, in single, semi-double and fully double forms. Some of the best known are **T. divaricata, (syn: T. coronaria) (Crepe Jasmine; Crepe Gardenia; Pinwheel Flower)**. This species is native from India to Yunnan and northern Thailand, and is known under many other common names such as East Indian Rosebay, Adam's Apple, Nero's Crown, and Coffee Rose. The glistening white flowers are set against dark glossy green leaves and are nocturnally fragrant. Very easy plants to grow and flower.

Thevetia — **(Yellow Oleander)** — A tropical American genus with approximately 8 species, the most popular of which is **T. peruviana (T. neriifolia)**. Popular throughout the tropical world for its ease of culture, lack of insect problems and attractive flowers it blooms in three prominent colors, white, orange, and bright yellow, with bright yellow being the most commonly seen.

Trachelospermum — A genus with about 20 species of evergreen vines native from India to Japan. The most popular for its intensely fragrant flowers is **Trachelospermum jasminoides (Star Jasmine; Confederate Jasmine)**, a wonderful vine whose flowers perfume the evening air as few others can. Easily grown and easy to bloom, the Star Jasmine vine is self-clinging and makes an excellent ground cover in warm climates or a fine specimen on a fence or trellis.

Urichites lutea (Yellow Mandevilla) — Another recent introduction of the mid 1990's with glowing yellow trumpet-shaped flowers. This vine of modest growth has glossy green leaves and is easy to grow and flower.

6

Plumeria obtusa var.
Matrimandir Gardens,
Auroville, India

Plumeria obtusa
Singapore

Plumeria obtusa var.
Matrimandir Gardens,
Auroville, India — note
pink bud

Plumeria caracasana
Wild collected in the
Dominican Republic —
Matrimandir Gardens,
Auroville, India

Plumeria (*Cacaloxochitl*)
found in the Badianus
Manscript, dated 1552,
depicting partially opened
flowers.

Plumeria stenopetala
(*P. stenophylla*)

Developing buds show-
ing color

First emergence of
inflorescence

Inflorescence showing
flowers and seed pods

NOMENCLATURE

The genus, Plumeria, was named after the French botanist, Charles Plumier (1646-1706), who was the pioneer systematist of the tropical New World flora. This interesting account is from Flowering Trees of the Caribbean: "The genus was named for Charles Plumier, the French ecclesiastic and botanist, who by appointment of the King of France, made three voyages to the Caribbean area in the seventeenth century. It was his countryman, and fellow botanist, Tournefort, who named the genus for him, since Plumier's records and drawings of West Indian natural life had earned him great respect from his colleagues. Tournefort originally spelled the genus Plumieria, but it is now often accepted as Plumeria."

CLASSIFICATION OF SPECIES

The Index Kewensis, originally funded by Charles Darwin, is the most complete enumeration of the genera and species of flowering plants and lists all the species names given to plumerias together with the author and publication in which it is to be found. Most of the listings are found in Tome II, by Hooker and Jackson, with further entries in the Supplements, the latest in Supplement X, 1936-1940, having only one listing.

Woodson's revision of the genus Plumeria (Annals of the Missouri Botanical Garden, 1938), recognizes seven distinct species with a few sub-species. He provides a key to the species and lists numerous synonyms described by previous authorities. It is interesting to note Woodson's comment while undertaking the revision: "An evaluation of the species of Plumeria by students unable to gain an extensive knowledge of the plants in the field, among whom the present writer must be counted, is attended by several difficulties. The first of these is the paucity of morphological characters in the flowers and fruits, the relatively few of which have been either unknown to most authors, or ignored by them."

The above statement reflects the need for a future study based on observations of living plants. Although Woodson's work is exceptionally thorough and his research included the examination of numerous herbarium specimens from European and American herbaria, the inability to study flower color and plants in bloom in a leafless condition as well as his own acknowledgement of the imperfections in a surprising number of herbarium specimens lead (50 years later), to the necessity of field study for

8

a modern revision. In <u>Hortus Third</u> (1976), only four species are currently described (based undoubtedly on Woodson's study), with descriptions of three additional forms of *P. rubra* listed.

Although much further data will be needed before authorities will concur on the exact number of species and the parentage behind the bewildering maze of hybrids, we do have a solid beginning with the above mentioned studies. One of our hopes is to have the opportunity some day to complete a definitive work on plumeria species and continue to explore the background of today's hybrids.

Woodson accords separate status as species to the following:

Plumeria inodora	— Colombia; British Guiana
Plumeria pudica	— Colombia; Venezuela; Martinique
Plumeria rubra	— Central America
Plumeria subsessilis	— Hispaniola
Plumeria obtusa	— Bahama Islands; Cuba; Jamaica; Hispaniola; Puerto Rico; locally in Yucatan and British Honduras
Plumeria filifolia	— Cuba
Plumeria alba	— Puerto Rico; Virgin Islands; Lesser Antilles

Since this is not a botanical treatise, we will restrict ourselves to non-technical descriptions of plants and flowers as an initial introduction to some familiar as well as lesser known species.

Plumeria alba

Producing white flowers with yellow centers, the habit of this species seems to vary considerably according to the area of the world in which it is grown. Raghuvanshi and Chauhan describe both a large flowered form and a smaller flowered form in their studies of the Apocynaceae in Lucknow, India. The variety described by Watson, Chinn, Clay and Brewbaker in Hawaii is obviously the small flowered form with flowers only an inch or so across. The leaves are light green and glossy, fiddle-shaped with rounded tips. The flowers are borne in loose clusters. The observation that seed pods rarely form on the small flowered variety is interesting since abundant pods form on the large flowered form though the seeds are mostly sterile.

The second form of *P. alba* has flowers to 2½ inches across, white with a tiny yellow eye at the base of the narrow, recurved and separated petals. The blossoms begin to turn brown a day after they are picked but are delightfully scented. The leaves, in contrast to the first form are dark, glossy green measuring about 7 inches in length and 1¾ inches wide. Dozens of mature specimens of this form of *P. alba* are to be found in sandy soil on the esplanade along the beach in Madras, India, where they grow to a height of 20 to 25 feet.

Plumeria obtusa

There are many variations in this species, each exhibiting unique qualities that set it apart from others. Many of the forms are so different in flower size and leaf shape that authorities have classified them as separate species. For example, one form of *P. obtusa*, previously known as *P. bahamiensis*, has unique lanceolate to linear-lanceolate leaves that often grow to 1 foot in length but only 1 to 1½ inches in width. Its white flowers vary from ¾ inch to 1½ inches across, are sparsely produced and mostly hidden within the foliage. This is a small tree with thin branches, usually not attaining a height of more than 25 feet. The follicles average 4 inches long by ½ inch across.

Plumeria obtusa var. obtusa
Most often called 'Singapore' in the West, its flowers are similar to the above but plants have a more spreading, umbrella-like form and reach 26 feet in height in Hawaii. Again, the flowers are intensely fragrant and borne in large clusters.

Plumeria obtusa var. sericifolia
Described by Woodson and <u>Hortus Third</u> as having the lower leaf surfaces, and often petioles and inflorescences, conspicuously pubescent.

Some of the forms we have studied (which may indeed prove to be separate species) are listed below:

P. obtusa var. — A distinctly dwarf form with a well branched, shrubby habit. This form is most popularly grown in containers throughout India and bears immense clusters of exquisitely scented white flowers with small yellow centers and wide, rounded, slightly overlapping petals. Flowers measure just over 3 inches across and petals are obovate.

P. obtusa var. — This variety is notable in many ways. Of all the obtusa forms we've studied, it has the largest leaves and flowers. The leaves are dark green but a shade or two lighter than the preceeding varieties described; they are oblong, averaging 12 to 14 inches in length and just under 3 inches across, with margins that curl upward to form a long "V" shape. Most extraordinary are the flowers which measure approximately 4½ inches across and are once again white and very sweetly scented but have narrow, very widely separated petals forming a large star.

P. obtusa var. — In this variety the dark green leaves are shorter, 11 to 12 inches in length, and wider, to 3½ inches across. The petals too are wider than the above, obovate, rounded and again widely separated. The most striking differences are lovely pink buds that contrast with the pure white flowers, and the sturdiness of the tree that grows to a height of 20 feet spreading to 25 feet with branches so thick and strong they can easily support the weight of a person. Again, the fragrance is enchanting and the flowers are large, 3½ to 4 inches across.

In recent years several remarkable hybrids with *P. obtusa* parentage have been introduced. According to Chinn and Criley in <u>Plumeria Cultivars in Hawaii</u>, one, 'Dwarf Singapore', is reported to be an F1 hybrid between 'Singapore' and 'King Kalakaua'. Another, 'Mele Pa Bowman', formerly known as 'Evergreen Singapore

Yellow', originated as a seedling with *P. obtusa* as one of the parents. A third, 'Iolani', is a hybrid between *P. obtusa* and *P. rubra forma acutifolia*. All are described in the chapter on Named Cultivars.

Plumeria filifolia syn. P. stenophylla

A very handsome shrub bearing masses of large, delicate, glistening white flowers with very narrow, widely separated petals borne in sparse clusters above and among the medium green, lanceolate leaves. This species was wild collected in the Dominican Republic. It is growing in Waimaea Arboretum on Oahu and was donated by Keith Wooliams to the Matrimandir Gardens in India. It would seem to have excellent breeding potential due to its dwarf habit, compact growth and ability to produce abundant seeds. Germination is excellent and seedlings appear vigorous and true to form.

Plumeria caracasana?

Although there is some question as to the correct name for this species, it is one of the most striking plants we have grown. This variety was also sent to the Matrimandir Gardens by Keith Woolliams from material wild collected in the Dominican Republic. It is so vigorous we were able to root and flower it in one year. Index Kewensis lists it in Supplement iv-1906-1910, (by J.R. Johnston in Contrib. U.S. Nat. Herb. xii 108 [1908].- Venez.). Woodson lists *P. caracasana* as a synonym of *P. pudica*. The most extraordinary aspect of the species is its enormous, pendulous flower clusters (to 18 inches across), that hang beneath the branches! The flowers are white, very large, easily to 6 inches across, with extremely recurved and widely separated petals that cascade downward like masses of ribbons. The dark green leaves are long and narrowly lanceolate.

Plumeria rubra

This is the progenitor of many of the beautiful named varieties we have today. *P. rubra* in its various forms, has supplied endless color combinations and exotic fragrances. Both Woodson and Hortus Third agree on four forms of *P. rubra*.

Plumeria rubra forma rubra

This is the typical form with the corolla predominantly rose of varying intensity and usually with a yellow center. This form is often found in Indian gardens today and is characterized by its heavy petal substance and the unforgettable scent of its flowers which is identical to the coconut hair oil often worn by Indian women or the coconut suntan oil more familiar in the West.

Plumeria rubra forma acutifolia (Poir.) Woodson
[Var. acutifolia (Poir.) L.H. Bailey; *P. acutifolia* Poir.; *P. acuminata* Ait.]

The above authorities and synonyms are cited as an example of taxonomic research, the many names a particular plant may have had, and the changes that occur when new information is developed or incorrect nomenclature is discovered. Synonyms are listed in a priority order so we see that *P. acuminata* Ait. is the last and least accepted, superseded by *P. acutifolia*, etc. All this to point out that this is the famous Frangipani flower with its legendary fragrance! In this form the corolla is white, usually with a prominent yellow center, sometimes flushed with rose.

Plumeria rubra forma lutea

This is a prominent species in Central America and Mexico with large flowers usually 4 to 4½ inches across. The branches, although strong, tend to bend and then curve upward again. Flowering is prolific with large, intensely fragrant, yellow blossoms fading to white at the edge as they mature. Woodson and Hortus Third note that the flowers are occasionally flushed rose or rose-pink on the outside.

Plumeria rubra forma tricolor

In this form the corolla is predominantly white, generally with a yellow center and the outer margins of the lobes rose-pink. Many of the "Rainbow" hybrids have this form in their background.

Plumeria pudica

As described by Woodson: "Leaves subsessile, obovate-oblong, more or less pandurate or cochleate; corolla lobes about half convolute in the bud, longitudinal in aestivation, or scarcely spiral; Colombia; Venezuela; Martinique."

Plumeria subsessilis

Again, described by Woodson: "Leaves subsessile, membranaceous, without a well-developed marginal vein, secondary and tertiary venation extremely pronounced upon both surfaces; flowers white 'with a yellow eye'; Hispaniola."

STANDARDIZED PLANT NAMES

The Standardized Plant Names for the genus as recognized by Hortus III are Frangipani and Temple Tree. The accepted common names for P. rubra L. are Nosegay and Frangipani. P. rubra forma acutifolia is known as the Pagoda Tree.

Nosegay is certainly apt, for what finer bouquet of sweet-smelling flowers could one have than a cluster of plumeria blossoms? Temple Tree and Pagoda Tree are traditionally recognized in the Far East. Frangipani, at least as widely known as all the others, has two fascinating derivations. Woodson, in his Studies In The Apocynaceae writes: "Although known under a variety of aboriginal names, the most widespread popular name for the cultivated Plumerias in use by Europeans is 'Frangipani' or 'Frangipanier'. Sir J.J. Smith (in Rees, 'Cyclopedia,' 1810), discusses the provenience of this name as follows: 'The French name of this genus, Frangipanier, is rather remarkable. It is said to allude to its fragrance, Frangipani being a sort of perfume so-called in France from its inventor, an Italian, of the Frangipani family, so conspicuous in the Roman disturbances of the twelfth century.'" Cowen adds: "'Frangipani' is undoubtedly the commonest name for all these trees, being associated with the very distinctive perfume. Four centuries before the discovery of the Western Hemisphere and of the trees growing there, an Italian nobleman, by combining a number of volatile oils, produced a heady perfume which became, and remained, a favourite with the noble ladies of Europe. This easily recognizable scent was at once recalled by the early settlers in the Caribbean when they found trees with the same fragrance. So they called them 'Frangipani', the name of the Italian nobleman." In <u>Flowering Trees of the Caribbean</u>, we find this similar explanation: "One day in Rome in the twelfth century, an Italian nobleman, taking time off from his official duties as bread-breaker of the Holy Sacrament to pursue his hobby, combined a number of volatile oils and pronounced the result his most tantalizing perfume. It proved to be a sure-fire formula and one that not only brought wealth to its makers, but fixed the inventor's name, which he had given the perfume, in the vocabularies of many nations. The man's name was Frangipani." The Frangipani perfume was of such an enchanting fragrance that it became the favorite of Catharine de Medici.

A second explanation for the common name, Frangipani, concerns the heavy white latex that flows freely from a cut in the tree. French settlers in the Caribbean area noticed this and termed it "Frangipanier" which is French for coagulated milk.

TRADITIONAL COMMON NAMES

There are literally hundreds of common names for the plumeria, some humorous or descriptive, others filled with spiritual meaning, and some woven into the religious or cultural fabric of a people. Here are a few of the more well-known.

Aztec	— Cacaloxochitl.
Australia	— Dead Man's Fingers
Brazil	— Jasmin de Cayenne
Central America	— Amapola de Venus
Columbia	— Azuceno, Floron
Dominican Republic	— Aleli
French Guiana	— Frangipanier
Guatemala	— Flor de la Cruz
Haiti	— Frangipani, Frangipanier
Hawaii	— Pumeli or Melia
India	— Temple Tree, Pagoda Tree
Indonesia	— Kamboja
Java	— Semboja
Mexico	— Suchil, Crow-Flower
Nicaragua	— Flor de pan
Philippines	— Kalachuchi
Puerto Rico	— Paucipan
Southern China	— Egg Flower
Salvador	— Flor de Mayo
Trinidad	— Frangipani
Venezuela	— Amapola, Atapaimo
Yucatan	— Flor de Mayo

The background of the name, 'Singapore', is interesting. Many years ago a plant of *Plumeria obtusa* was brought to Singapore from the New World tropics. Years afterward a plant was taken from Singapore to Hawaii. From then on *P. obtusa* has been known as 'Singapore' in Hawaii and on the mainland!

Plumeria rubra forma acutifolia is known as Graveyard Flower or Common Yellow in Hawaii and elsewhere as Frangipani.

There is a mental projection when you give a precise meaning to a flower. In can answer, vibrate to the contact of the projection, accept the meaning, but a flower has no equivalent for the mental consciousness. In the vegetal kingdom there is a beginning of the mental consciousness. In the animal it is different: the mental life begins to form and for them things have a meaning. But in the flower it is something like the movement of a baby—it is neither a sensation nor a feeling, but something of both; it is a spontaneous movement, a very special vibration. If you are in contact with it, if you feel it, you can get an impression which may be translated as a thought. That is how I give a meaning to flowers and plants. There is a kind of identification with the vibration, a perception of the quality that it represents. Little by little, through a kind of approximation that sometimes comes all of a sudden and on other occasions needs time, there occurs a close approach between these vibrations, that are of the vital-emotional order, and the vibration of mental thought. If there is sufficient accord, you have a direct perception of what the plant may signify.

The Mother

Slaughter Pink

Unnamed cultivar —
Matrimandir Gardens

Paul Weissich

Penang Peach

Iolani

Courtade

Madame Poni

Pauahi Alii

3

HISTORICAL DATA

DISTRIBUTION AND CLIMATIC RANGE

Plumerias are indigenous to the New World Tropics, from southern Mexico to northern South America, especially the islands of the Caribbean. Due to their popularity and ease of culture, plumerias have been introduced into all tropical areas of the world and one can see more varieties today in gardens in Singapore, India, and Hawaii than in their native habitats. Plumerias are true tropicals and will not tolerate much cold. They are not found at elevations above 3000 feet in South India where the tropical heat gives way to the cooler, more temperate climate of the higher elevations, but have been recorded in the New World tropics up to 3900 feet.

Although they thrive in hot, dry climates plumerias are very adaptable and can be seen in high rainfall areas, in varying soil conditions, from mountains to sea level, but always in full sun exposure.

On the mountainsides of Guatemala, plumerias grow in poor soil and tolerate a hot, dry climate. They may be found along the Nile, in many parts of Africa, in the tropical areas of Australia and along the coastal belt of Southern California. I have travelled through miles of thorny scrub jungle in South India to suddenly come upon a large specimen of *Plumeria rubra acutifolia* rooted in the crevice of a huge boulder, thriving in blistering 100 degree heat where there is often no rain from January through July! This is true as well in certain areas of Mexico such as Oaxaca where plumerias are found in arid, barren areas growing together with cactus. In <u>The Vegetation of Peten</u>, the author writes: "In April and May, *Plumeria acutifolia* strikingly stands out on the hill sides with its beautiful large white flowers." And this in an area where there is a layer of humus so thin that it barely covers the larger roots of many of the trees! We have seen plumerias in the wet country of Hilo, Hawaii, and on the opposite end of the island of Hawaii in Kona, a hot dry region where plumerias are planted along the roads in pits dug out of lava! Whether on mountainsides, in the crevices of rocks, along sandy beaches or in lava formations, plumerias may survive poor soil but it must be soil that is well-drained.

Eliovson mentions that plumerias stand the sea-breeze well and grow magnificently in Durban, South Africa. An article in the August, 1986, issue of <u>Sunset</u> magazine suggests that in desert areas some afternoon shade helps, but left alone in nature plumerias seem able to tolerate almost anything.

As to plumerias being brittle and easily broken, this is true in their early years but in tropical areas they rapidly develop strength and elasticity and are able to grow under very difficult conditions, having been known to withstand hurricane winds. Plumerias in seaside gardens even develop tolerance for salty air without undue damage to their leaves.

INTRODUCTION OF SPECIES AND HYBRIDS

Plumeria cuttings can survive for weeks and even months if properly handled and so have been transported around the world and introduced by plant collectors to the major gardens of the world. We have seen specimens in the greenhouses of Kew, on the rooftops of penthouses in New York City, and in fact, everywhere we have travelled.

Plumeria rubra forma acutifolia, the Common Yellow Frangipani, was introduced into Hawaii by William Hildebrand in 1860. Harold Lyon brought the first cutting of *Plumeria obtusa* into Hawaii from Singapore in 1931 and, according to Watson, Chinn, Clay and Brewbaker, it is still growing at Foster Garden in Honolulu today. *Plumeria rubra* was brought to the Hawaiian islands in the early 1900's. Joseph Rock mentions that, "The first specimen [of *P. rubra*] was brought to Honolulu from Mexico by Mrs. Paul Neumann . . .". *P. alba* was introduced from India and *P. bahamiensis* (now a form of *P. obtusa*) from Nassau were introduced to Hawaii as late as the 1950's.

Clarissa Kimber in Martinique Revisited writes: "Frangipani (*Plumeria rubra*) from Mexico or Central America was an early garden introduction (Labat 1742, . . .)."

In his 1906 book Indian Trees, Dietrich Brandis makes an interesting comment about *Plumeria acutifolia*: "A native of Mexico and Guatemala, cultivated in India from time immemorial."

In fact, in The Ornamental Trees of Hawaii, written by Joseph F. Rock in 1917, we find the following: "The Plumeria is now cultivated in many tropical countries as an ornamental tree. It was found in India growing abundantly as long ago as 1787 by a Dr. Hove."

As to other species and hybrids, during the 1970's we introduced to India through the gardens in Auroville many of the Hawaiian and Singapore varieties along with several from Mexico, and as previously mentioned, the species from the Dominican Republic.

The introduction of Plumerias continues today through exchanges by botanical gardens around the world and through mail order sources. New named varieties are much in demand, especially dwarf forms, as are new forms that have developed their own distinctiveness in places as far away as Africa, Australia and India, in addition to those resulting from breeding work in Hawaii and on the U.S. mainland.

MEDICINAL, ECONOMIC AND DECORATIVE USES

There are numerous references in literature to the medicinal uses of plumeria latex and blossoms reaching as far back as the Badianus Manuscript, the 16th Century

Aztec Herbal. Helen O'Gorman notes in <u>Mexican Flowering Trees and Plants</u> that: ". . . the flowers of the 'cacaloxochitl', or raven-flower, were used with other ingredients in a potion to be drunk as a remedy 'for fear or faint-heartedness'. The juice of the plants is used sometimes in the treatment of wounds, and in Yucatan the extract is said to be employed in the treatment of cutaneous and venereal diseases. The latex is said to produce a good quality of rubber."

George Watt, in his <u>Dictionary of the Economic Products of India</u>, mentions a number of uses for plumerias in India. Some of the more important are described as follows:

> The sap is employed with sandalwood oil and camphor to cure itch, and is used as a counter-irritant to cure rheumatic pain. The bark, known as A'chin, is recommended by the Persians as a cure for gonorrhoea and venereal sores. It is used for a similar purpose in Puerto Rico. In Bombay, it is used for intermittant fevers as we use Cinchona. In the Konkan, it is given with coconut, ghee and rice as a remedy for diarrhoea. A decoction from the bark makes a powerful anti-herpetic. Its use as a purgative is not without danger, however. Several cases of death from excessive purging after its use have been recorded. Plasters made from the bark are said to be useful in dispersing hard tumors.
>
> The leaves, after being heated, are applied as a poultice to reduce swellings. In Goa, the leaves and branches are tied around coconut palms to protect them against the attacks of the Long-horned Beetle (*Batocera rubra*).
>
> The flower buds are taken with betel leaves as a febrifuge. The seeds, when available, are boiled in milk and given as an antidote in cases of snake bite. Mr. Millard once had a few seed-pods on one of the trees in his garden in Bombay and his Mahratta malis [gardeners] expressed the belief that the seeds were eaten by cobras. The seeds certainly disappeared, but he had his suspicion that the malis were in league with the cobras.

Blatter and Millard quote the following from Mhaskara and Caius in <u>Some Beautiful Indian Trees</u>: "Both the bark and the fruit are useless in the antidotal and symptomatic treatment of snakebite; the fruit is also useless as an external application to the part bitten."

Watt also gives a preparation for a purgative under the heading, Special Opinion: "This plant is known as Dalana phula in Northern Bengal, where its milky juice has been tried and found to be an effectual purgative. The dose is as much as a grain of parched rice (khai) will absorb, the grain being administered as a pill. (Surgeon Major C.T. Peters, M.D.)."

Francis Perry writes in <u>Flowers of the World</u>: "The English explorer, Henry Bates, who in 1848 explored hitherto unknown reaches of the Amazon, wrote in <u>A Naturalist on the Amazon</u>, 'One of the most singular of the vegetable production of the campas is the Sucu-u-ba tree (Frangipani) . . . The bark and leaf stalks yield a copious supply of milky sap, which the natives use very generally as a plaister in local inflammation, laying the liquid on the skin with a brush and covering the place with cotton. I have known it to work a cure in many cases.'" Perry also writes that the Javanese make sweetmeats from the flowers. (Note: according to Woodson, the Sucu-u-ba tree is not a plumeria but a totally different genus, Himatanthus, though both exhibit certain similar qualities such as showy flowers, copious milky white latex, etc.)

In Hawaiian Plumerias the authors state: "The white, soft, light wood is used to make drums in India; harder, more mature trunks of the trees are used in the Caribbean area for making bowls, trays, cabinets and furniture."

Kunkel adds the following in Flowering Trees in Subtropical Gardens: "According to Burkill a decoction of the bark is given in Indonesia for venereal diseases, and the milk is purgative and used as a counter irritant for toothache or when dropped into sores. The plant is used to cure intestinal disorders in horses. . . ."

From Flowering Trees of the Caribbean: "The Frangipani is too small a tree to have much timber value, but the wood still has been put to many local uses. A yellow-brown with faint purplish streaks, it is hard, heavy and compact. Craftsmen who make from it bowls, cabinets and small furniture find it easy to work, lustrous and good for a high polish."

Many books refer to the corollas being used as sweetmeats and a remedy for cough.

Although the above is fascinating reading, today the most familiar economic use is of the flowers in decorations, arrangements and leis (garlands). In Hawaii, the creation of leis has become an art form and annual exhibitions are held to select the most novel and creative displays. Here are a few suggestions on making leis. Use a long needle (in Hawaii they have a "lei needle"!) and white thread or thin monofilament line (4 lb. test is sufficient). The flowers may be strung end to end or sideways through the base of the petals if a fuller lei is wanted. A well made lei will have 40-60 flowers. When you are through stringing the flowers, knot the two ends and you are finished. To make a tighter lei, shorten the ends of the corolla tubes. Some leis are made of individual petals and may contain thousands of petals. You may extend the keeping quality of flowers by soaking them in water for about 15 minutes then draining off the excess water and storing in a plastic bag in the refrigerator. Leis will keep for several days in this manner.

RELIGIOUS AND CULTURAL SYMBOLISM

In tropical countries plumerias are among the most loved of all flowers. In Hawaii they are made into leis and presented on all special occasions. Visitors arriving in Honolulu are traditionally given the greeting of a lei, often made entirely of plumerias of various colors or of plumerias in creative combinations with other flowers. In Mauritius and the Seychelles, arriving visitors are greeted with leis and in the evenings, candles surrounded by plumeria flowers are floated in pools, exuding a fragrance that is intoxicating and unforgettable. In the Far East plumerias are planted around temples and the flowers are given as offerings to the gods. Cowen writes in Flowering Trees and Shrubs of India: "To Buddhists and Mohammedans the tree is an emblem of immortality because of its extraordinary power of producing leaves and flowers after it has been lifted from the soil. For this reason it is frequently planted near temples and in graveyards, where daily the fresh, creamy blooms fall upon the tombs. Hindus make use of the flowers in worship and they are frequently given as votive offerings to the Gods." This is a custom in countries as far apart as India and Hawaii. We have often passed by ancient Muslim cemeteries and been treated to the sight of clouds of white flowers floating on a sea of dark green leaves of *Plumeria obtusa*.

This ability of plumerias to survive for months without sustenance, especially unrooted branches, broken or pruned from trees was described by W.M. Thomas of Citronelle, Alabama, in a letter to us in September, 1988. Mr. Thomas writes, "This year I decided to prune it back [his plumeria tree] but did it in stages. I gave some of the cuttings away and there were 2 left which I tossed on the ground and never got around to picking up for the trash. The cuttings were outdoors and the grass grew over them because I couldn't get the mower that close to them. Since July we have had good rain but I forgot about the cuttings. Imagine my surprise when I discovered the cutting actually lying on the ground had rooted along the stem and was now in full growth." (Mr. Thomas later wrote that the roots appeared to have formed along the stem but had actually developed only at the cut end.)

In the Philippines the plumeria is known as Kalachuchi and has the same duality of symbolism found in other countries, traditionally used in mourning and planted at gravesites but also very popular in garlands.

A neighbor in Houston, Texas, while taking a walk one day past our house, stopped to share with us the interesting fact that in Southern China plumerias are called Egg Flowers, since the most common variety there is white with a yellow center.

A friend, Is Moritis, originally from Central Java and now a resident of Houston, has shared with us the many symbolical and traditional uses of the plumeria in different areas of Indonesia. Is relates many fascinating stories of the plumeria including its name which for some unknown reason is Kamboja to the Indonesians and Semboja to the Javanese, both terms indicating that the flower came from Cambodia. The most common variety is *Plumeria obtusa* (not called 'Singapore' in Indonesia!), which is planted primarily in cemeteries. Java has 80 million people in an area one-seventh the size of Texas. Burial land is therefore very difficult to find. Legend has it that you are very lucky and especially loved by God if you get a burial plot under a plumeria tree where one may find eternal rest in its shade. The flowers falling on the tombstones indicate that the Divine Providence takes care of the departed and sees that fresh flowers bedeck the grave each day. The plumeria is, therefore, a very special plant filled with spiritual meaning, and for this reason not planted around the home. During the past 20 years a number of hybrids have found their way into the front yards of residences but *Plumeria obtusa* in Central Java (which is influenced by Animism and Mohammedanism as well as Hinduism and Buddhism) retains its spiritual meaning.

Marco and Teresita Lopez, who are from Merida, Yucatan, and now live in Houston have recently shared some beautiful traditions of the plumeria with us. In the Yucatan the plumeria is called Flor de Mayo, the flower of May. May is the month of the Virgin Mary and the plumeria is dedicated to Her and treated with great respect as a religious symbol. During this month, when plumerias are in full bloom, the children go to church each day dressed in pure white, the girls in white veils as well. At the altar is an immense wooden "M", in honor of the Virgin, drilled throughout with small holes. During the mass each child enters the church with a basket of plumeria flowers of different colors and while singing, walks up to the altar and places one flower in the "M". The children continue this all through the mass which lasts about 45 minutes and at the end, the "M" is ablaze with the beauty of plumerias. Each day the mass is held in a different church and the ceremony repeated by the children. Due to the strong religious symbolism, plumerias are rarely worn in the hair; the white butterfly ginger being more favored for this use. This offering to the Virgin Mary in May is also performed in Taxco.

Woodson writes: "The fragrance, as well as the abundance of waxy, beautifully tinted flowers, apparently caused the Plumerias to be prized by the Indians long before the advent of the Spaniards, and garlands are still used in tropical America as nosegays and head-dresses and to decorate the altars."

According to Matschat, the "Cacaloxochitl" or Crow-Flower, *Plumeria rubra forma acutifolia*, was a favorite of the ancient Mexicans and much prized by the Aztec maidens of the nobility who wore them in their hair.

In Flowering Trees of the Caribbean, the author notes that it is practically a ritual to perfume rooms and linens with Frangipani blooms before the visit of an honored guest in Batavia. (Possibly a reference to Dutch colonies? Ed.)

Waterfield eulogizes the plumeria in one of his ballads:

Well have our fathers done,
Tree of the silent one
Still in thy praise shall the story be said,
Well did they, choosing thee
First of the wood to be
Watcher and guard of the graves of the dead.

Others are fairer trees,
Waving along the breeze
Bending with mourners the wanweeping head.
Rough and uncouth thy form,
Steadfast before the storm
Pointing to heaven from the graves of the dead.

Others have brighter hue,
Heaven's own starless blue,
Purity's white, and affection's deep red.
Thou with thy blossoms pale
Scented the evening gale
Hallowing with incense the graves of the dead.

Others their treasures cast
After the bloom is past,
Withered and scentless the gifts that they shed.

Thou while thou flourishest
Giveth thy first and best
Strewing thy buds o'er the graves of the dead.

Therefore thy name we praise
As in former days
When on the tombs, thy first of rings were spread.

Forest flowers by day
Thou shalt unwearied lay
Sentinels sure at the graves of the dead.

We conclude with a quote from Dr. T.A. Ramakrishnan in a letter of Nov. 7, 1979: "Plumeria and Peace go in company and there is nothing to beat this beautiful plant for achieving tranquility and utter peace of mind."

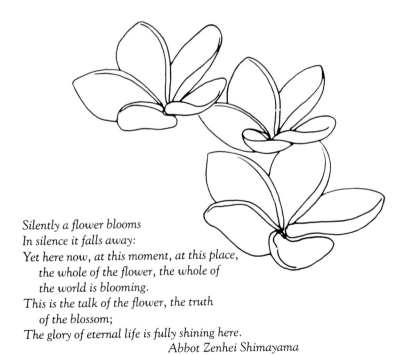

Silently a flower blooms
In silence it falls away:
Yet here now, at this moment, at this place,
    the whole of the flower, the whole of
    the world is blooming.
This is the talk of the flower, the truth
    of the blossom;
The glory of eternal life is fully shining here.
                    Abbot Zenhei Shimayama

Scott Pratt

Kauka Wilder

Donald Angus

Celadine

Irma Bryant

Schmidt Red

Hilo Beauty

Moragne Red

Angus Selection

Kona Hybrid

A mature plumeria tree growing in Hawaii. Height approximately 10-12 feet with twice that in spread. Note the tall Araucarias (Norfolk Island Pines) in the background.

One of many dense compact shrub-type plumerias in a natural habitat with a carpet of ferns beneath and the blooms of the Octopus tree (Brassaia actinophylla) in the background.

DESCRIPTION

PLANT TYPES AND STRUCTURE

Plumerias range in size from dwarf shrubs that even in the most ideal climates rarely grow more than 3 to 4 feet in height after many years, to large trees that may attain heights up to 40 feet with an equally impressive spread. *Plumeria obtusa* and its varieties are primarily evergreen while most of the other species are briefly deciduous in their native habitats.

In the more desirable species and cultivars, growth habit is compact with multiple branching and dense foliage in whorls at the ends of the branches, and crowned by large inflorescences. Immature branches are green and soft, almost succulent, shiny, and in some varieties lightly pubescent. Mature wood is gray and characterized by prominent leaf scars. In some species the leaf scars are so prominent that the bark appears warty. In most species and hybrids the bark is smooth and though it is occasionally thick, cork-like and furrowed, leaf scars are always evident to some degree. Branches have some elasticity but in young plants will not sustain weight and break easily. Mature trees develop much greater strength and it is possible to climb near the top of 30 foot specimens without breaking a limb.

As to the structure of the plants, we have come across some rather unique descriptions. Cowen writes: "Although rarely without flowers, it is leafless from December until the rains and, beautiful though the flowers may be, they cannot conceal the ugliness of the pale swollen limbs."

Here is a description by Menninger from his <u>Flowering Trees of the World</u>: ". . . an awkward set of wooden antlers topped with nosegays. The gouty, soft-barked trunk and the gray, non-tapering branches that are more conspicuous than the foliage, make it the ugly duckling of the tropical garden. It is saved from oblivion only by the exquisite and often heavy fragrance of its waxy flowers which rival both the Jasmines and the Gardenias."

From Firminger's <u>Manual of Gardening for India</u>: ". . . not ill-looking when in full foliage, with its large, lanceolate, smooth leaves, nine inches long and two and a half wide, borne, crowdedly, towards the summits of the stems, but remarkably uncouth when the succulent, gouty-looking stems are destitute of leaves, as they often are in the cold months."

In <u>Some Beautiful Indian Trees</u>, Blatter and Millard write: "In full leaf the tree is not without elegance, but stripped of its handsome foliage, its crooked trunk and the grotesque outlines of its blunt and swollen branches give it an uncouth and gouty appearance."

Colthurst, however, in Familiar Flowering Trees in India, achieves a balance, seeing beauty evolve from the beast:

> It is a small, gouty-looking tree, which is often leafless but rarely out of bloom, with thick, smooth branches that do not taper at all, and are full of a tenacious white milk.
>
> For all its fragrance, the Frangipani are not exactly what one would call artistic trees, and time was when I vigorously excluded it from my garden, but one day I came upon Waterfield's eulogy of it in his "Ballads" [See Religious and Cultural Symbolism], and now, for the very beauty of his ideas and the music of the poem it is one of my favorites.

In The Modern Tropical Garden, Kuck and Tongg also write in a more positive tone: "One of the most popular and attractive of smaller flowering trees with picturesque form and flowers useful for many purposes. . . . Flowers which appear on the bare tree, in large clusters near branch ends, create a particularly picturesque effect."

As we can see from the above, no botanist, horticulturist or tropical plant enthusiast who has written anything descriptive about plumerias has minced words when giving a detailed account of the rather awkward, ungainly form of the plant with its swollen looking branches, greyish scarred bark and angular branching structure. All are equally unanimous, however, in their appreciation of the abundant and often spectacular bouquets of fragrant flowers that cover the plant for many months of the year. The plumeria does have its champions and a few even see beauty in the form, which can be highly architectural with its bold sculptured lines and forked branches supporting tufts of leaves above which are held the magnificent clusters of perfumed flowers.

Taylor writes in his Encyclopedia of Gardening: ". . . very handsome shrubs and trees . . .", and T.M. Greensill in Tropical Gardening makes a fine statement: "Generally, this small tree is not given the attention it deserves. A well-tended specimen has branches about a foot from the ground and is perfectly symmetrical in shape, with the lower leaves almost sweeping the ground. . . . A well-shaped specimen is one of the most beautiful sights in the tropics. . . ."

GROWTH HABITS AND LIFESPAN

With the exception of the dwarf varieties most plumerias grow rapidly, easily attaining 2 to 3 feet a year in tropical areas under favorable conditions. In the southern and western states, plants often grow at least 1 foot per year with good culture. Though some seedlings and uncultivated varieties exhibit undesirable characteristics such as tall spindly growth with sparse branching and inflorescences so high one needs a ladder to appreciate the flowers, in better varieties branching occurs at close intervals and growth is symmetrical. During the development of an inflorescence at the tip of a branch, latent buds immediately beneath will begin to initiate growth and branches will emerge and continue to grow throughout the flowering period. In some varieties only 1 or 2 branches are typical, but in more vigorous types at least 3 or even as many as 5 or 7 will develop. Each new branch leads to a potential inflorescence in the next 1 to 2 years. Plumerias are very long-lived plants. The original *Plumeria rubra forma acutifolia* introduced by Hildebrand to the Foster Botanic Gardens still grows where it was planted 128 years ago. Even older specimens are reported to be alive and flowering in Mexico.

LEAVES

Plumeria leaves are arranged alternately and are crowded near the ends of the branches. The leaves of different species and hybrids exhibit considerable variation (see Appendix A) in shape, size, color and density. In general, leaves are thick, stiff, leathery and light to dark green in color with a well developed mid-rib and a distinct intramarginal vein that connects the prominent lateral, feather-like veins that run at right angles to the mid-rib. The leaves of *Plumeria obtusa*, for example, are a rich dark green, obovate to obovate-oblong, with rounded tips and thick mid-rib and lateral veins. Leaf sizes range from 5 inches in length to some we have measured at more than 20 inches and vary from ½ inch across to nearly 6½ inches at the widest point. Most species and hybrids are glabrous but a few are moderately pubescent.

INFLORESCENCE

Flowers are produced on terminal thyrsiform inflorescences that usually rise well above the foliage providing a mass display that is incomparable. A few species and sub-species produce their inflorescences among the leaves and one, *P. caracasana* (specific epithet doubtful) bears huge clusters beneath the foliage. Some inflorescences, such as those of cultivar 'Japanese Lantern', are initially upright and become pendulous as they mature. We have often observed inflorescences with 20 to 30 flowers open at one time on plants grown in the ground under good cultural conditions. Yet, many of today's modern hybrids will produce almost the same number of blooms on container grown plants only 2 to 3 years old!

FLOWER SHAPES, SIZES AND COLORS

Flowers are generally medium to large though there are small flowered species and hybrids. The corolla is salverform with 5 lobes convolute in bud and a slender corolla tube. Stamens and other reproductive parts are not visible, being inserted deep within the corolla tube. There are 5 stamens borne on the corolla, the anthers separate and free from the short 2-lobed stigma, pistil with 2 half-inferior ovaries and a single, spindle-shaped style. Flowers are usually very showy and fragrant, in a range of hues with white, pink, yellow and red the representative colors, although many new hybrids have beautiful orange, golden and salmon shades with a few hybrids definitely tending toward lavender. There is often a deeper band of red, rose-pink or pink on the reverse outer edge of the petals. The inner margin of the lobe curls inward. We have observed variations in the number of lobes from 3 to 7, with a few hybrids displaying 6 lobes on 50% of the blossoms.

Individual blossoms are most often 2 to 4½ inches across in hybrid forms, with some varieties approaching 6 inches. Shapes range from large star-shaped blossoms with very narrow, widely separated petals to tightly overlapped, saucer-shaped forms, and every conceivable variation in between. Some flowers have a pinwheel shape with the corolla lobes pointed and reflexed while others have rounded lobes. In other hybrids the corolla lobes may be twisted or undulate (see Appendix A).

Flower color may vary according to the conditions under which a plant is grown. We have observed flowers shading to lavender rather than pink when grown under fiberglass. Plants flowered in too much shade will also be far from their true color. Flowers on immature plants such as second or third year seedlings as well as first year cuttings may not be true to color or size.

FLOWERING SEASON AND HABIT

In Hawaii the heaviest flowering season extends from April through October. In Southern California plants bloom from June through November (nearly that long in the southern and southeastern states) and occasionally into December. In most of the tropics P. obtusa is almost perpetually in bloom. Flowering habit varies greatly according to climate and habitat. Menninger writes: "In Florida the trees are leafless in spring when flowering begins and the flowering may continue for months. New leaves gradually appear as the blossoms drop away." T.H. Everett in the New York Botanical Garden Encyclopedia of Horticulture writes: "In climates with a definite dry season they usually flower when they are leafless, but in constantly moist climates they are likely to be evergreen and bear flowers and foliage at the same time." In Flowering Trees of Guatemala, Chickering observes: "The traveler who passes through the Motagua Valley during the spring or early summer will see, rising among the dry shrubs and cactus along the roadside or the railway, occasional small trees surmounted by large clusters of glistening white flowers. Early in the season the trees are often leafless. . . ." In India mature trees of P. rubra forma acutifolia begin to drop their leaves with the onset of the heavy rains, remaining leafless for 6 to 8 weeks. The period of heaviest bloom is January and February, in a leafless condition, and in March when the new leaves burst forth.

Steiner writes that the 'Red Kalachuchi' (Plumeria rubra), blooms from February to November in the Philippines while the 'White Kalachuchi' (Plumeria obtusa), blooms throughout the year. O'Gorman writes, referring to P. rubra forma acutifolia in Mexico: "The leaves . . . usually do not appear until after the blossoms in spring." She continues: "In Acapulco many of the white flowered species grow in the surrounding hills. Here, as in the tropical zone of Papantla, the flowers appear together with the foliage and not on bare branches, and the blossoms can be seen as late as July."

FRAGRANCES

The plumeria is synonymous with perfume. According to Woodson, Jacquin described the odor as ". . . perhaps the sweetest of any plant living,. . . ." "Only the bloom of the jasmine with which it is so often identified can compete in sweetness and penetration of scent." (Flowering Trees of the Caribbean). Miller and Hubbard write in The Standard Cyclopedia of Horticulture: "Plumerias are among the most fragrant of tropical flowers, vying in this respect with the jessamine, Cape jasmine and tuberose."

Plumeria flowers are most strongly scented during the evening and in the morning and fragrance is faintest during the heat of mid-day. Fragrance in plumerias is a study unto itself and should be thoroughly researched. No other flower seems to be possessed of so many different and intoxicating perfumes. Though one occasionally finds a flower that is odorless or only mildly scented, most plumerias have strong and wonderful fragrances, variously described as citrus, coconut, rose, cinnamon, honeysuckle, jasmine, gardenia, lemon, fresh peaches and other aromatic fruits. The Frangipani fragrance is associated only with the widely cultivated species, *Plumeria rubra forma acutifolia*, a medium size white flower with a prominent yellow center.

Overall, as a group, the plumerias we grew in India seemed to be the most highly scented, often exquisitely so. We noticed this same phenomenon with oleanders as well. Whether this was due to the type of soil, the sun, water, fertilizing or other unknown factors, we do not know. In Auroville we conducted an interesting experiment with a group of school children ages 4 to 13 who came weekly to the Matrimandir Gardens to study plants and Nature. We evolved a game of identifying flowers while blindfolded, by their scent alone. The children took this challenge quite seriously and were delighted when they learned to identify many different flowers by their characteristic fragrance. After a time they were able to distinguish at least twelve distinct plumeria fragrances.

Each time we visit Hawaii, or perfumeries in other places, we always hope we will find a plumeria perfume that truly captures the essence of the plumeria fragrance. There are numerous companies producing 'Plumeria' perfumes, but to date we have been disappointed in the results. Senor Frangipani must have found the secret and kept it closely guarded.

FOLLICLES AND SEEDS

Seed pods, or follicles, are produced in abundance in some species and many hybrids and take about 8 months to mature. Follicles are usually stout and appear in pairs (typical of the Apocynaceae family) though occasionally only one will form. They are easily noticeable on the trees, are of smooth texture and brown to reddish-brown in color. For more information on seeds refer to the chapter on Propagation.

Puu Kahea   Kimi Moragne   Dwarf Singapore

Kaneohe Sunburst   Kimo   Lurline

Cindy Moragne   Cerise   Sally Moragne

5

MAJOR CULTIVARS

The following list describes nearly 60 named cultivars presently in cultivation. Of the thousands of plumeria hybrids throughout the world, these have been selected for a number of reasons. Firstly, almost all are recognized varieties, documented in various publications, and known in cultivation for many years. Most, though not all, are also commercially available, an important consideration. Lastly, they are proven performers, having been selected through years of testing in home gardens and experimental research stations for their unique attributes of size, color, fragrance, length of flowering season, size of inflorescence, keeping quality, etc. For ease of reference they are listed by predominant color.

WHITES

'Daisy Wilcox' — Very large, creamy white flowers with a prominent yellow center and pale pink buds. Flowers open with a faint pink blush and quickly fade to white. Individual blossoms measure up to 4½ inches across and have wide, floppy petals, ". . . better for wearing in the hair than for lei making. . . ." (Chinn & Criley), with a charming light pink band on the reverse of the broad, rounded, heavy-textured petals. Flowers have a spicy fragrance, good keeping quality, and are borne in large, dense clusters. Parentage: *P. rubra forma acutifolia.*

'Dwarf Deciduous' — One of the most beautiful of the modern hybrids. Large white flowers, intensely perfumed, have broad, oval petals and a golden center. Flowers average about 3 inches across and are borne in many-flowered inflorescences. A larger plant than 'Dwarf Singapore', but a true dwarf; of easy culture, very compact habit and continuously in bloom from spring through fall, even into winter in mild climates. Nearly evergreen; leaves drop briefly and reappear almost immediately.

'Dwarf Singapore' — This is a rare, dwarf form of the famous 'Singapore', *Plumeria obtusa,* and is possibly a cross between *P. obtusa* and "King Kalakaua'. Chinn and Criley remark: "This unique new low-growing cultivar resembles a shrub, with many small, cupped flowers in tight clusters. Insects are not usually a problem. It is recommended for home gardens. Released by Department of Horticulture, College of Tropical Agriculture, 1970." 'Dwarf Singapore' is a many-branched plant that is perfect for small spaces, and like 'Dwarf Deciduous', can be flowered indoors.

Keeping quality of the flowers is good, leaves are semi-glossy and flowers have a lemon fragrance.

'Elena' — Pure white flowers with a large, brilliant yellow center and a narrow pink band on the back. Petals are wide with a pointed tip and moderately overlapping. Flowers have a mild sweet fragrance, heavy texture, and keeping quality equal to that of the best, 'Celadine'. Plants have a long blooming season. Parentage: *P. rubra forma acutifolia*.

'Hausten White' (**'Willow's White'**) — Large white flowers, 3½ to 4 inches across, with a small, brilliant yellow center and medium pink bands on the back. Petals are wide with round tips, moderately overlapping with a heavy texture and a sweet fragrance. Upright, densely branching plants with moderate to heavy flower production. Parentage: *P. rubra forma acutifolia*.

'King Kalakaua' (**'Miniature White'**) — Small white flowers have a brilliant yellow center and a fragrance similar to gardenias. Petals are wide with a pointed tip, moderately overlapping, of medium texture and good keeping quality. Parentage: *P. rubra forma acutifolia*.

'Samoan Fluff' (**'Tahitian White'**) — Striking, round, full petals are white with a small, brilliant, greenish-yellow center and medium pink bands on the back. Petals are highly overlapping and of good texture. Flowers are 3½ inches in diameter, have very good keeping quality and a strong, sweet fragrance. *P. rubra forma acutifolia* is one of the parents.

'Sherman' (**'Polynesian White'**) — Large flowers, 4½ inches in diameter, are white with a large, brilliant yellow center (no color bands on front or back); have fair texture, a slight sweet fragrance and poor keeping quality. Plants make large symmetrical trees with dense branches. Parentage: *P. rubra forma acutifolia*.

'Singapore' — This is the species, *Plumeria obtusa*, mentioned so often in other chapters. Flowers have the famous Frangipani fragrance and are pure white with a small, brilliant yellow center and no color bands on front or back. Flowers average 3½ inches in diameter. Plants are densely branched with glossy, dark, evergreen foliage.

YELLOWS

'Aztec Gold' — Large, buttercup yellow flowers, 3½ to 4 inches across, have a faint pink band on reverse that is barely noticeable when the flower is fully open. The edges of the petals fade to white with age. Plants are free-blooming with branches that bend, then sweep upwards again. Possibly a pure form of *P. rubra forma lutea*. Possessing a heady, strong fragrance of fresh peaches, this variety is easily flowered and has a long season of bloom.

'Bali Whirl' — The world's first double flowered plumeria with ten petals. Flowers are medium to large with spreading petals that make one flower look like a small cluster! The flower size and color is similar to 'Celadine', a rich bright yellow with the edges of the firm petals bordered white. This cultivar may indeed be a sport of 'Celadine' as it blooms freely and is very easily grown.

'Celadine' — Known in Hawaii as **'Common Yellow'** and **'Graveyard Yellow'**, and in Singapore and Thailand by the much more beautiful name, 'Celadine'. Flowers are medium to large, to 3½ inches across and brilliant yellow, usually with a broad white margin around the firm textured petals. Strong Frangipani fragrance (some say lemon scented), with very good keeping quality. Parentage: *P. rubra forma acutifolia*.

'Gold' (**'Peterson's Yellow'**) — Brilliant yellow flowers with a narrow, white margin around the wide petals which are moderately overlapped with the margin rolled inward. Good texture and keeping quality combine with a pleasant lemon scent. Flowers contrast nicely with the dark green leaves. Parentage: *P. rubra forma acutifolia*.

'Iolani' — This rare cultivar is almost impossible to acquire but is listed in Plumeria Cultivars in Hawaii. The flowers are 4 inches in diameter, brilliant yellow with narrow, pale yellow margins that fade very little. Petals are long and wide with rounded tips, very slightly overlapping, and of moderate texture. The background of the common name is quoted from the above publication: "Named in honor of Iolani Luahine, Hawaii's high priestess of the hula and the mele. Permission granted by Iolani Luahine, November 1978. Released by Department of Horticulture, College of Tropical Agriculture and Human Resources."

'Mele Pa Bowman' (**'Evergreen Singapore Yellow'**) — This hybrid between *Plumeria obtusa* and 'Celadine' bears large, highly fragrant, yellow blossoms edged in white. Plants are evergreen with large, glossy, deep green leaves. It is named after the mother of Maile O'Donnell, who accidently bred the plumeria in her yard.

PINKS

'Angus Selection' (aka **'Giant Plastic Pink'**) — This new introduction of the early 1990's features very large hot-pink flowers with broad, rounded petals, darker pink upon opening, then aging to a lighter pink. All shades appear in the cluster at the same time. Flowers emit a sweet, enchanting fragrance.

'Courtade Pink' — A Houston introduction from Edward Courtade in 1975, the large flowers average 4 to 4½ inches across, and occasionally exceed 5 inches. Flowers are a medium pink with a lavender tint and a prominent yellow center; petals rounded and slightly overlapped. Plants flower easily and produce large inflorescences. Flowers have an enchanting "lavender" fragrance. A hybrid of unknown origin.

'Grove Farm' — A very large, spectacular, lavender-pink flower with a small, brilliant yellow center. Petals are rounded, heavily overlapped, and covered with fine, darker pink lines. Flowers measure 4½ inches across, have a sweet "old-fashioned" fragrance, heavy texture and good keeping quality. Flower production is moderate to heavy and plants bloom for 8 months in tropical areas. Parentage: *P. rubra* and *P. rubra forma acutifolia.*

'Kimi Moragne' — Very large, sweetly fragrant, intense rose-pink flowers shading to lighter pink at the extreme edge of each petal and a golden-orange center. Petals are very round and overlapping. Clusters are large and dense with many flowers open at a time. A cross of 'Daisy Wilcox' and 'Scott Pratt'.

'Mary Moragne' — Creamy blush-pink flowers are shaded darker on one edge, with fine, orange lines extending from the golden-orange center. Flowers are very large with oval petals and a refreshing, sweet fragrance. Inflorescences are immense and flower production is excellent. Very easy to flower, this cultivar also sets seeds readily. A cross of 'Daisy Wilcox' and 'Scott Pratt'.

'Mela Matson' — Abundant clusters of medium pink flowers with a small, orange-yellow center and wide, rounded, overlapping petals that are reflexed, forming a cup shape. The fragrance is delightful; sweet with a slight lemon accent. Flowers are usually a minimum of 3 inches in diameter during the warmest months and bloom over a long period. A hybrid of *P. rubra* and *P. rubra forma acutifolia.*

'Moir' — Delicate pink flowers have a delightful citrus fragrance, wide elliptical petals with pointed tips, and a broad, deep pink band on the reverse. Flowers are 3¼ inches in diameter and of good keeping quality on this long-flowering cultivar. Parentage: *P. rubra forma acutifolia.*

'Plastic Pink' — Also known as 'Royal Hawaiian', this cultivar has vibrant, hot-pink flowers with a strong red band on the back, wide, moderately overlapping petals, very good keeping quality and flowers profusely. Plants tend to branch easily and bloom for many months. Parentage: *P. rubra.*

'Sally Moragne' — Large flowers open a soft, peachy pink with a golden center and fade to white with pink shading at the edges of the petals. Both colors are present in the clusters at the same time, creating a lovely two-tone effect. Petals are angular and overlapping like pinwheels. A cross of 'Daisy Wilcox' and 'Scott Pratt'.

'Tillie Hughes' — A favorite for its lovely, soft creamy pink flowers with deeper shading on one edge of the petals, and a glowing orange-yellow center. The petals are moderately overlapping with a medium pink band on the reverse. Flowers are 3¼ to 4 inches in diameter, sweetly fragrant, and produced in abundant clusters. Flower production is moderate to heavy on this densely branched cultivar. *P. rubra* is one of the parents.

PINK AND WHITE

'Carmen' — Sweetly fragrant flowers are pink suffusing to white with a bright yellow center and a strong red band on one edge of the reverse, making the buds appear red. Petals are wide and overlapping with heavy texture; keeping quality is excellent. Flowers average 2½ to 3 inches in diameter. Seed set is excellent and branching is dense. Parentage: *P. rubra* and *P. rubra forma acutifolia*.

'Espinda' — Wide, oval, overlapping petals are soft pastel pink with a golden yellow center and deep pink bands on the reverse. Good texture, good keeping quality and prolific bloom are trademarks of this cultivar. Flowers are sweetly fragrant and average up to 3¼ inches in diameter. Parentage: *P. rubra forma acutifolia*.

'Loretta' — Flowers average 2½ to 3 inches in diameter and shade from pink to white with deep pink streaks radiating from the brilliant yellow center. Good keeping quality and good texture with an interesting grainy pigmentation are features of this long flowering cultivar which posseses an extraordinary fragrance somewhat like Gardenias. *P. rubra forma acutifolia* is one of the known parents.

'Maui Beauty' **('Manoa Beauty')** — Abundant clusters of lemon scented, 3¼ inch flowers are pink with a bright yellow center and wide, rounded petals. Broad, strong pink bands on the reverse create a striking contrast between flowers and buds. Heavy texture and very good keeping quality further distinguish this cultivar. A hybrid of *P. rubra* X *P. rubra forma acutifolia*.

'Moragne #23' — This is the largest flower in the Moragne group, 5 to 6 inches in diameter; a soft-textured, creamy white shaded from the center with a rich gold and suffused with pink from the pink band along the back edge of each petal. Petals are broad and slightly recurved. A tiny red spot marks the center of the flower. Buds are also pink and flowers mass together in enormous, dense clusters. A cross of 'Daisy Wilcox' and 'Scott Pratt'.

'Ruffles' **('Vanda')** — With distinctive, wavy petals resembling Vanda orchids, the sweetly fragrant flowers are 2 inches in diameter, pink with a large, radiant yellow center and deeper pink bands on both front and back. Texture and keeping quality are fair. Plants are densely branched and suitable for landscaping in warm climates. Parentage: *P. rubra* X *P. rubra forma acutifolia*.

'Slaughter Pink' — A prolific cultivar bearing immense clusters of delicately shaded flowers with narrow, pointed, reflexed and separated petals of pastel pink and soft yellow fading to white. Easily grown and flowered, it has a strong, sweet, citrus fragrance and is a good seed bearer. The parentage of the hybrid is unknown.

'Tomlinson' — One of the best varieties of all. Wide, rounded petals have distinctive, fine white lines radiating into a lovely shade of pink on the outer edges and a small, glowing yellow center. Sweetly fragrant flowers are 3 inches in diameter, have fair texture with very good keeping quality and are borne abundantly on densely branched plants. In Hawaii the cuttings root easily in loamy soil. A hybrid of *P. rubra* X *P. rubra forma acutifolia*.

'White Shell' — A very unusual cultivar with white flowers banded red on one edge of the reverse of the petals. Flowers have a golden-yellow center but in cooler weather only open partially and resemble seashells. Texture is good and keeping quality is very good; fragrance is strong and sweet. This is a hybrid of unknown origin.

RAINBOWS

'Candy Stripe' — Recently introduced in the late 1980's, this cultivar is a striking blend of white, red and yellow stripes. Other distinguishing characteristics are its ability to root quickly, its vigour and a tendency to produce multiple branches.

'Kaneohe Sunburst' — Large, deep pink flowers are 3¾ inches across and have a large, brilliant yellow center. Petals are streaked with radiating red and yellow lines with a strong red band on the reverse. Flowers have good texture and fairly good keeping quality; fragrance is sweet, and both flower and seed production are heavy on this densely branched cultivar. *P. rubra* is one of the parents.

'Kona Hybrid' — An outstanding cultivar of the early 1990's, this is an exciting new variety with large, waxy 3-4 inch flowers in a pastel rainbow combination of peach, pink and yellow with a tinge of lavender. The plants produce large clusters of flowers with rounded overlapping petals. Plants flower easily and prolifically.

'Lei Rainbow' — A unique blend of rainbow colors—pink, yellow and red—with separated petals, make this a very popular variety in Hawaii and more recently in the U.S. Blooms in large clusters and is one of the easiest to flower. Cuttings root easily and will often flower as they are rooting.

'Madame Poni' (**'Star'**, **'Corkscrew'**, **'Curly Holt'**, **'Waianae Beauty'**) — A challenge to categorize, this is one of the most incredible shapes of all plumerias. Flowers are large, 3½ inches in diameter, with narrow, curved and fluted petals that are white with a greenish-yellow band that extends down the middle of each petal and sienna-red stripes within the bands. Petals are widely separated and have strong red bands on the back. Good texture, good keeping quality, sweet fragrance and no known pests or insect problems add to its allure. A hybrid of unknown origin.

'Nebel's Rainbow' — Large, brilliant yellow flowers with a red band on the front and back of each petal. Petals are wide with rounded tips and a moderate overlap. Texture is heavy and keeping quality very good. Flowers are 3½ inches in diameter and have a mild, sweet fragrance. Flower production is heavy on strong branches. This is a hybrid of unknown origin.

'Peachglow Shell' — One of the loveliest and most delicate of the unusual plumeria flowers. Most notable is the fact that the flowers open only partially, giving the appearance of sea shells by displaying the reverse of the petals which are banded with rich pink on one edge gradually changing to creamy white. As the flower begins to open (never fully in Hawaii but often in hot summer climates), it reveals the glowing, golden inner petals. The texture of the petals is heavy and the strong, sweet fragrance is enchanting. Keeping quality is excellent. Parentage: *P. rubra forma acutifolia*.

'Puu Kahea' ('O'Sullivan', 'Fiesta') — A truly superior flower, brilliant yellow with a strong red band on both front and back of petals. Individual blossoms are very large, just over 4 inches in diameter, and have a tangy lemon fragrance with good keeping quality. Parentage: *P. rubra* X *P. rubra forma acutifolia*.

GOLD

'Paul Weissich' (OP #3 Gold) — Named in honor of the director of the Foster Botanic Garden in Honolulu in 1987, the strong golden yellow flowers have an orange center with pinkish-orange lines radiating into the center of the petals. Flowers are 3 inches in diameter with wide, rounded, highly overlapped petals. Keeping quality is good and the fragrance is mild and sweet.

'Pure Gold' — A rare cultivar that we have seen in Hawaii and have acquired to test for ourselves. Flowers are the purest solid gold, very sweetly fragrant, approximately 2½ to 3 inches across, of good substance and keeping quality. Hybrid origin unknown at this time.

'Pauahi Alii' ('Angus Gold') — This plant, formerly listed as 'Angus Gold' should now be 'Pauahi Alii'. Dr. Criley has written: "We received a request for a cultivar to name in honor of Bernice Pauahi Bishop (last heir of the Bishop Estate lands and the person for whom the Bishop Museum is named), and they selected this plant from among many that Donald Angus had collected (the name Angus Gold was merely an accession name in our field plots). The name the Bishop Museum requested was 'Pauahi Alii'." The large, brilliant gold flowers have wide, dark red bands on front and back and a dark red center. Flowers are 3¼ inches in diameter, of heavy texture and very good keeping quality, and have a fine lemon fragrance. Parentage: *P. rubra* X *P. rubra forma acutifolia*.

LAVENDER-RED

'Keiki' ('Miniature Lavender') — This is a small flower, a moderately strong red suffused with lavender overtones and is therefore potentially valuable for future hybridizing work. Flowers are 2 inches in diameter with wide, elliptical petals with pointed tips, moderately overlapping, of fair texture, fair keeping quality and a slight spicy fragrance. A hybrid with *P. rubra* in its background, it is cultivated for its semidwarf nature (another possibly advantageous trait).

SALMON PINK TO ORANGE

'Dean Conklin' — Very large, breathtakingly lovely flowers with a glowing golden center. Oval, pointed petals shade from light pink on one edge to deeper salmon-pink with a red band on the reverse. Flower color may occasionally exhibit deeper pink shadings but in full sun is basically salmon. Individual blossoms often average 4 inches and more across and have a spicy scent similar to carnations. This is a selection from Donald Angus' collection and, quoting Criley and Chinn: "Named for the late Dean Conklin, plant enthusiast and member, Board of Directors for Friends of Foster Garden. Released for the 1977 dedication of the Dean Conklin Plumeria Grove in Koko Crater Botanic Garden by Department of Horticulture, College of Tropical Agriculture." Plants are vigorous and flower production is very heavy. Parentage is *P. rubra forma acutifolia* hybrid of unknown origin.

'Jean Moragne' — Immense flowers to 5½ inches across, almost orange on opening and changing to pink at the edges of the petals when mature. Petals are slightly pointed creating a lovely star shape. A hybrid of 'Daisy Wilcox' and 'Scott Pratt'.

'Kauka Wilder' — This extraordinary flower is an intense combination of yellow and red creating the appearance of a fiery orange bloom. Petals are narrow and slightly overlapping with a pointed tip. Flowers average 3 inches across and have an especially strong, sweet fragrance. One of the earliest and easiest to bloom, it also ranks among the most highly perfumed of all plumerias. Parentage is *P. rubra*.

'Kimo' — A magnificent flower. The glowing apricot-orange blossoms have a strong pink band on the reverse and the wide, rounded, heavily overlapping petals nearly form a complete circle. Flowers average 3 inches across, have a very heavy texture, good keeping quality and a sweet, fruity fragrance. This is a seedling from 'Gold' and was released by the Department of Horticulture, College of Tropical Agriculture, University of Hawaii, in 1970.

'Lurline' - A striking combination of bright red-orange on yellow with a reddish star at the center. The tips of the petals and the outer margins are purplish-red. The heavily textured flowers are large, to 4 inches in diameter, and have a spicy fragrance. Flower production is heavy and continues for many months. According to

Criley and Chinn, it is: ". . . an open-pollinated seedling of 'Gold'; sibling to 'Kimo'. It was named in honor of and with the permission of Mrs. Lurline Matson Roth." Released by the Department of Horticulture, College of Tropical Agriculture, University of Hawaii, in 1973.

RED

'Cerise' — This cultivar produces large clusters of star-shaped flowers with a tiny, golden-yellow center and narrow, slightly overlapping, elliptical petals with a distinct twist, especially towards the tip. Flower color is intense magenta to moderate red. Individual blossoms average just over 3 inches and have a sweet permeating fragrance. *P. rubra* parentage.

'Donald Angus' — An excellent cultivar producing large clusters of flame red flowers with a large orange-yellow center and strong red bands on both front and back. The wide, oval petals are of heavy texture and are moderately overlapped. Flowers average 3 inches in diameter, have very good keeping quality and a delightful fragrance. Parentage is 'Common Yellow'. Introduced by the Department of Horticulture, College of Tropical Agriculture, University of Hawaii, in 1970.

'Duke' — Flowers are large, to 3½ inches across, with strong red and pink hues. The wide petals moderately overlap, have a rounded tip and a strong red band on the front. Flower production is very heavy and continues over many months. One of the most fragrant flowers, becoming even more fragrant when picked. Parentage: *P. rubra* X *P. rubra forma acutifolia*.

'Hilo Beauty' — Dark, velvety red, star-shaped flowers with wide, elliptical petals that slightly overlap. The reddish-brown to purplish bands on front and back create a very dark red appearance. Keeping quality is excellent, one of the best! Flowers are large, 3½ to 4 inches in diameter with a spicy fragrance that increases after picking. The largest of the strong red cultivars. Parentage is *P. rubra*.

'Irma Bryan' — A true red variety with uniquely shaped petals, broad at the base with a distinctive notch at one corner. Petals are moderately overlapping and have slightly wavy edges. Flower size is 2½ inches in diameter. The spicy aroma of the blossoms becomes even stronger when picked. Plants tend to be upright and closely branched. Parentage: *P. rubra*.

'Japanese Lantern' ('Flower Basket') — Vibrant, rose red flowers with a small but intense yellow center. The petals are narrow and elliptical with a pointed tip that recurves. Flowers are 3 inches in diameter and have a mild, sweet fragrance. Flower production is very heavy and the large inflorescences become pendulous in time, hence the common name. A very long-blooming variety. Parentage: *P. rubra*.

'Katie Moragne' — The most striking and intensely colored of all the Moragne hybrids. An unusual, vibrant brick red that is strikingly contrasted with the soft white of the rolled inner edge of each petal. A hybrid of 'Daisy Wilcox' and 'Scott Pratt'.

'Moragne Red' — Very large flowers to 5 inches across, carmine red fading to pink with soft gold, and fine red lines radiating from the center of the flower. Petals are very round, overlapping and slightly cupped. Sweetly fragrant. A hybrid of 'Daisy Wilcox' and 'Scott Pratt'.

'Scott Pratt' (**'Kohala'**) — Unusually deep red flowers with deep purple-black veins and a wide, dark, purple-brown stripe on the reverse. A very long blooming variety producing until late in the season. Flowers are of heavy substance, average 3 inches across, have excellent keeping quality and a sweet fragrance reminiscent of coconut oil. Parentage: *P. rubra*.

'Schmidt Red' — One of the newest and best of the deep red hybrids. Flowers are large, of good substance, moderately overlapped and have excellent keeping quality. A true, deep red, the individual blossoms average at least 3 inches across. Parentage: *P. rubra*.

William M. Moragne

Mrs. Lillian Upchurch wearing a plumeria lei containing 1800 petals.

Dr. Richard A. Criley with seedlings from The Matrimandir Gardens at the Waimanolo research station.

Mary Moragne (Mrs. Samuel A. Cooke) and the "Mary Moragne" Plumeria.

Mary Helen Eggenberger and a magnificent plumeria on Kauai.

PLUMERIA IDENTIFICATION CHECKLIST

NAME: _____

(include species, variety or cultivar)

PLANT DESCRIPTION:

Medium shrub (3-6 ft.) _____   Small tree (to 21 ft.) _____

Large shrub (6 + ft.) _____   Medium tree (21-48 ft.) _____

1. Height (at maturity) _____   Spread (at maturity) _____
2. Circumference of trunk at base (2 ft. above soil) _____
3. Shape: Dense rounded _____ Open _____
4. Bark: Rough _____ Smooth _____ Fissured _____ Knobby _____

    Green _____ Grey _____ Brown _____
5. Evergreen _____ Deciduous _____
6. Rate of growth: Fast _____ Average _____ Slow _____
7. Flowering: Prolific _____ Medium _____ Poor _____
8. Length of significant bloom per season (weeks) _____
9. Size of flower cluster (inches diam.) _____

    a. How borne: Above foliage _____ Among foliage _____ Pendulous _____
10. Age: Cutting _____ Seedling _____

LEAF DESCRIPTION:

1. Length _____ Width _____
2. Tip: Rounded _____ Pointed _____ Elongated _____
3. Shape: Lanceolate _____ Acuminate _____ Spatulate _____ Obvate _____
4. Color: Light green _____ Medium green _____ Dark green _____

    Yellow green _____ Other _____
5. Thickness: Thin _____ Medium _____ Thick _____
6. Margins: Wavy _____ Straight _____
7. Texture: Dull _____ Glossy _____ Leathery _____ Pubescent _____
8. Habit of growth: Opposite _____ Alternate _____ Whorled _____

    Ascending _____ Descending _____ Lateral _____
9. Veining: Primary: Feather _____ Lateral _____

    Marginal: Distinct _____ Indistinct _____

    a. Color: Red _____ Green _____ Yellow _____ Bronze _____
10. Petiole: Length _____

    a. Color: Light green _____ Green tinged brown _____ Reddish brown _____

FLOWER DESCRIPTION:

1. Color (Predominant): (circle choice below)

    a. White   b. White with pink   c. White with yellow   d. White with gold

    e. Yellow   f. Yellow with white   g. Gold   h. Light pink   i. Magenta

    j. Dark red   k. Pastel rainbow   l. Strong rainbow   m. Pastels (peach,

    apricot, etc.)   n. Tints
2. Shading: Upper surface _____ Margin _____

    Under surface _____ Margin _____

3. Color of eye _____ Color of throat _____

4. Monocolor _____ Bicolor _____ Tricolor _____

5. Size: Tiny (less than ½ in.) _____ Small (½ - 2 in.) _____
   Medium (2 - 3½ in.) _____ Large (over 3½ in.) _____

6. Shape: Rounded _____ Star _____ Pinwheel _____ Cupped _____
   Salver _____ Reflexed _____

7. Petal Shape: Rounded _____ Pointed _____ Narrow _____ Twisted _____
   Oval _____ Obovate _____ Recurved _____ Incurved _____ Ruffled _____

8. Petal separation: Heavy overlap _____ Slightly separated _____
   Slight overlap _____ Widely separated _____

9. Pedicel:
   a. Color: Green _____ Reddish _____ Other _____
   b. Length _____

10. Fragrance: Faint _____ Medium _____ Strong _____
    Citrus _____ Jasmine _____ Rose _____
    Fruity _____ Spicy _____ Coconut _____ Other _____

11. Substance: Light _____ Medium _____ Heavy _____

12. Texture: Waxy _____ Velvety _____ Glossy _____ Pubescent _____

13. Bud: Color _____ Shape _____ Size _____

14. Color variation as flower ages: None _____ Minor _____ Significant _____
    Color intensifies _____ Color fades _____

15. Lasting quality: Excellent _____ Good _____ Fair _____ Poor _____

SEED POD:

1. Color _____

2. Shape: Straight _____ Curved _____ Hooked tip _____

3. Size (length in inches) _____

4. Average number of seeds per pod: _____

SEEDS:

1. Size (including wing) _____

2. Color _____

SPECIAL CHARACTERISTICS:

1. Bloom: Early _____ Mid-season _____ Late _____

2. Seed set: Excellent _____ Fair _____ Poor _____

ADDITIONAL OBSERVATIONS:

_____

_____

_____

_____

_____

_____

Ellen #15 — One of the many spectacular cultivars under trial at various testing grounds in Hawaii.

THE MORAGNE HYBRIDS

A significant breakthrough in plumeria hybridizing was made by the late Bill Moragne, former plantation manager for Grove Farms Sugar Company on Kauai. Gardening was a lifelong hobby for the Moragnes, and Bill and his wife, Jean, grew numerous anthuriums, hibiscus, heliconias and plumerias.

Bill Moragne's daughter, Mary, has kindly shared with us all the publications she could gather on her father's work in controlled hybridization. We quote her own words from an article published in the <u>Garden Club of America Bulletin</u>, Vol. 63, No. 2, April 1975, entitled "A Special Plumeria".

Twenty five years ago while my father William M. Moragne Sr. was manager of Grove Farm Plantation on Kauai in Hawaii, he had a very interesting thought. How do you cross-pollinate plumerias? He knew that small insects helped pollinate the flowers, but that process was only occasional. He could find no written records on how to cross-pollinate plumerias, and no one he talked to knew how to go about it. He decided to experiment.

Since the plumeria gives off so much milky juice when cut, he immediately ran into trouble. Another obstacle in his experimentation was that the pistil is located at the very base of the flower. How was he to get the pollen all the way down the very thin stigma and style?

He wanted to cross the large light pink, . . . (Daisy Wilcox), plumeria that grew in his yard with pollen from the dark red Scott Pratt. He tried various techniques, including cutting off the leaves and flower petals to make them bleed before putting pollen on the pistil. This was to prevent the milky sap from getting into the cut when he was trying to cross-pollinate. In order to get down near the pistil, he made a diagonal incision into the base of the flower, exposing the small green pistil with pollen grains above it. He removed all the existing pollen, being careful to get all the dust out, and placed pollen grains from the <u>Scott Pratt</u> on the pistil. He then sealed up the incision with tape and waited . . . and waited . . . but nothing happened.

He could not understand why there weren't more seed pods produced naturally, let alone by his experimental method, because the pollen was so close to the pistil. Finally he decided that the pollen tubes must go down the side of the pistil, because nothing happened when he put the pollen on top. By putting the pollen under the edge of the pistil, he found the secret to success. Four seed pods began to develop and in about three months they were mature and ready to plant in seed boxes.

From four pods, 283 seedlings grew. They were transplanted into cans and, in approximately three months, they were ready to go into the seedling nursery. They grew there until they flowered, some within three years and others not until they were almost twenty years! He culled out all the duplicates or ones with poor flowers. One had flowers a foot in diameter with petals almost as narrow as a pencil! The blossoms ran the gamut of colors from white all the way to dark red. All had a pink edge on one side of the back of the petal.

Besides the collection in his own garden on Kauai, he added to the collections of the Foster Garden in Honolulu and the University of Hawaii. He also planted his new seedlings along both sides of the Nawiliwili Road for about a mile, interspersing them with kukui trees.

He chose thirty-five of the best flowers—those that would make the most durable and beautiful lei flowers and named his seven favorites for the girls in his family with Moragne names—Jean (his wife), Mary, Sally, Katie (his daughters), Jeannie (his son's wife) and Cindy and Kimi two grandaughters (his son's daughters). All the rest were given numbers.*

My plumeria, the Mary Moragne, is growing in our yard in Manoa and has lovely large pink flowers with yellowish centers. How many daughters have such a clever father who could develop a new new floral variety and name it after her!

*I asked my father if he registered the information. He said, "No, there was no plumeria society."

In addition to the excellent article by Mrs. Samuel A. Cooke we have some personal notes from Jim Little from conversations with Bill Moragne:

Pollination Information Demonstrated by Wm. Moragne

Wm. only pollinated the first thing in the morning and chose newly opened flowers. He used a small brush or forceps and pollinated underneath the edge of the pistil (not the top).

He used his pocket knife to make a slit (incision) in the lower middle of the flower.

He then covered the pollinated area with plastic tape rather than use a plastic bag.

Seeds appeared within the first month.

Eleven months later he picked the mature open pod.

The seedlings flowered in 4 years.

Little continues in another article: "I was doing some photography for Donald Angus, who has collected plumeria plants from all over the world. He knew I was interested in hybridizing, and he introduced me to Bill Moragne. Bill taught me how to hand pollinate. . . ."
Hopefully the above information will encourage an entire generation of plumeria hybridizers to achieve wonders in a field that has barely been touched.

"Beautiful gardens are fine things, but the fierce addiction of gardeners goes far beyond pretty pictures made with plants.
A fellow who delivers the mail has written me that he must have seen pretty gardens—he guesses—but it was only when he became a mailman, late in life, and traveled by foot, that he began to notice the great differences that exist among roses.
Leisure, slowness, contemplation: in an age of presumed efficiency and professionalism, these amateur virtues are perhaps despised but they may under-lie the greatest joys of gardening, and of life. It is not enough to grow the most beautiful things. It is even better to explore them, to identify with them, and to grow into a rather new consciousness of them . . . ."

Henry Mitchell,
The Essential Earthman

Tillie Hughes	Dean Conklin	Daisy Wilcox
Dwarf Deciduous	Dwarf Deciduous	Japanese Lantern
Tomlinson	Aztec Gold	Mary Moragne

7

NEW AND DWARF VARIETIES

NEW VARIETIES

As we travel to different areas of the tropics each year we continually collect and evaluate new plumerias. Through our plant exchanges we have been fortunate in acquiring rare hybrids that are now under cultivation and study. One of these is reported to be the world's first double, 'Bali Whirl'. Another, 'Petite Pink', is truly a rare treasure. It is extremely compact in habit, densely branched and bushy, with small but lush dark green leaves like that of *P. obtusa*. In fact, we believe it to be a variety of *P. obtusa* as it is also evergreen. In addition to all these wonderful characteristics, it is also covered with tight clusters of the most delicate white blossoms flushed pale pink with pale pink buds. This is the first dwarf to appear exhibiting color and will be an ideal container plant.

In the coming years we will be working with hybridizers and collectors in different parts of the world with a view towards introducing new varieties that have not been seen in the U.S. thus far. We have recently learned of varieties in Africa, Australia, New Zealand, and some of the Caribbean Islands that are totally different from all the wonderful ones we have collected to date! Future work will concentrate on three major areas: methods of propagating the rarest cultivars in greater quantity so they will become accessible to more people; development of more dwarf varieties for container culture; research into developing hybrids that will have a greater range of cold tolerance.

DWARF VARIETIES

The increasing popularity of plumerias and the necessity of growing them in containers in so many areas has convinced us that dwarfing should become the major emphasis for the future. At the present time there are few dwarf varieties and these are in very limited supply. We have described 'Dwarf Singapore' and 'Dwarf Deciduous' as well as 'Petit Pink' in other chapters, and these are basically the only dwarf forms known in cultivation.

We look forward to the advent of more dwarf varieties (and hope that this work will be a part of our own research in the near future), as breeders realize the potential that exists in color, shape, form and fragrance when plumerias can be cultivated as compact container plants.

Larva of the long-horned beetle, *Lagocheirus obsoletus Thoms.* in the stem of a plumeria.

Long-horned beetle, *Lagocheirus obsoletus Thoms.*

Long-horned beetle on a plumeria branch — note area that has been chewed

Rust pustules of *Coleosporium dominguense* appearing on the underside of a plumeria leaf

Black tip fungus that has killed new growth and completely inhibited further development

A fascinating anomaly — the appearance of new leaf growth from a prior inflorescence

Stem taken from parent plumeria plant rooted in water. Note root nodes beginning to develop.

Same stem shown later. Note development of roots and continued health of cutting.

One year later, plumeria cutting with extensive root system in water only. A small amount of fertilizer was added throughout the year.

Photo courtesy of George Slusser

8

PLUMERIA CULTURE

Plumerias are among the world's easiest plants to propagate, grow and flower. They are so easy, in fact, that we know of no other plant that will give so many months of fragrant and colorful rewards for so little effort. This section is devoted to sharing our knowledge and that of many of our friends to assure you of success in all areas of plumeria culture. We have files full of letters telling us how easy they are to grow. One of the most illuminating is from Marcia Todd Romberg of Austin, Texas. We quote excerpts from her letter of July 1986 to open this section:

> I have grown plumerias in Austin and Dallas for more than twenty years and have never had one fail to bloom prodigiously all summer, have any insect or other problems, or any cutting fail to grow and bloom. . . . I have real difficulty in convincing the people I give these to that they are the easiest plant in the world to grow. Whenever they have failed it was because people won't believe me and give too much loving care.
>
> Mine are set out (either in the ground or in pots) after the last possible frost date (usually about April 1 here). They are put into ordinary garden soil (Austin's is highly alkaline) with lots of compost. During the summer they get only the routine lawn watering and since we are almost always on water rationing here that can be only every five days. They bloom heavily all summer and frequently set seed although I have never grown any from seed.
>
> When a few of the leaves begin to turn yellow in the fall (and always before November 15) the plants (which have incredibly small root systems for their total size) are lifted with whatever soil clings and set into plastic garbage bags and set into a garage heated only by the presence of the hot water heater. No watering all winter.
>
> You <u>said</u> you wanted to hear of other grower's delight—of frustrations I have none.

PROPAGATION

Plumerias may be propagated from seeds, cuttings, air-layering or grafting. All methods assure you of success, but the first two are the easiest.

Seeds

The seed pods of plumerias are correctly known as follicles and somewhat resemble two downward curving horns. In tropical areas follicles ripen throughout the year but are most abundant in spring. They should be allowed to ripen as fully as possible on the tree which takes up to eight or nine months. In temperate climates, follicles (hereafter called pods for simplicity), often break off before maturity since their stems often do not have enough strength to hold them. This is especially true of plants grown in containers. If you would like to propagate seeds from one of your plants be sure to support the weight of the ripening pods with a plastic tie.

It is interesting to note that we have never seen a pod break off in the tropics. No doubt the longer growing season and the fact that plants are in the ground are contributing factors toward stronger plants. If you do have one break off before it has fully matured, allow it to ripen in a warm, dry place. If it splits open or dries enough for you to split it open, feel the seeds inside. If the seeds are plump and there is no evidence of fungus attack, there is a good chance they will be viable. One can often save pods in this way, especially if they are within a month or so of ripening.

When a pod splits open it will reveal perfectly aligned rows of seeds. Remove the soft, cork-like endosperm tissue and lift out the seeds. Each seed is covered with a tough, membranous brown sheath with a papery wing of the same size or larger. The seeds will lay in overlapping rows beginning from the tip of the pod. Half a pod may contain more than 50 seeds!

Some plumerias rarely develop pods, others produce numerous pods with sterile or mostly sterile seeds (this was true of *Plumeria alba* in India), and some produce a very high percentage of viable seeds. Plumeria seeds can remain viable for more than a year under good storage conditions and sometimes for 2 to 3 years.

An interesting discovery was made by Elizabeth Thornton who sprayed gibberelic acid on newly emerging flower buds (⅛ to ¼ inch high) and found that seed set increased.

Testing for Viability

Take a seed between thumb and forefinger and squeeze it lightly. It should feel plump and solid to the touch. After discarding flat and dessicated seeds, select at random from among the remainder and cut one or two open. If the embryo is cream-white and fleshy the seeds are viable, if dry and hard, or brown, they have lost their viability.

Planting Media for Seeds

In the tropics we planted seeds in a light, porous, fully sterilized medium. We sifted compost, added sand and topsoil, mixed all the ingredients in proportion and then sterilized. Here in the U.S. things are so much easier. One can purchase any number of quality potting soils already sterilized and pre-mixed. These are generally lightweight "soilless" formulations containing sphagnum peat moss and perlite, (occasionally some vermiculite), to provide good aeration and drainage with just the right amount of moisture retention.

There are a few important keys to success. Seed trays need only be 3 to 4 inches deep but must have plenty of holes for drainage. One of the most important things to remember is to moisten the planting medium thoroughly prior to planting the seeds. This is necessary because mixes high in peat generally do not accept water readily or evenly unless a wetting agent has been previously added to the mix. Place seed trays in morning sun or filtered light for best germination.

Successful Germination

One of the real secrets of success, both for germinating seeds and for rooting cuttings, is soil temperature. A cold, damp soil does nothing to encourage germination of seeds or root formation in cuttings and often has the effect of rotting both. Be sure the soil is warm before attempting to germinate plumeria seeds. An ideal temperature is around 80 degrees. During the past three years we have made a number of experiments with bottom heat (see paragraph on Planting the Cutting), and can report an unqualified success with both seeds and cuttings. We have also used grow-bulbs approximately 6 inches above the soil with excellent results.

Planting the Seeds

Following are three methods for planting plumeria seeds:

Method 1:
This method has proven successful for many growers in temperate and subtropical climates. Plant seeds with the wing upright and completely out of the soil, as if the seed had dropped down to earth and embedded itself only to the depth at which the wing begins.

Method 2:
This is a simple method that has also proven quite successful. Lay the seeds between two thicknesses of moistened paper towels. As soon as the seeds germinate they may be transplanted into small individual containers.

Method 3:
This is the best method we have found for successfully germinating plumeria seeds. Plant them horizontally about ⅛ inch deep, or about twice the thickness of the seed. Planting too deep inhibits germination and planting too shallow causes the seeds to rise to the surface. Perhaps the best rule-of-thumb is the salt and pepper analogy—even if you pour on the salt and pepper, it will never be more than a light coating! After covering the seeds, firmly tamp the medium. The importance of good soil contact cannot be overemphasized. Give seedlings plenty of room; preferably 2 to 3 inches apart.

Watering Seeds and Seedlings

Damp-off, a fungus that attacks and destroys young seedlings with extreme rapidity, is caused by overwatering and crowding of seedlings by planting seeds too close together. Plumeria seeds are not especially prone to damp-off, but as a general rule, one should be careful about watering too much and planting too close. In fact, more plants are killed by TLC (over-watering is first in this category), than any other cause! Since the medium has been thoroughly moistened before planting, a light sprinkling should be sufficient to keep the soil damp until germination. The finer the spray the better so as to disturb the soil as little as possible. Once the seeds have germinated, water moderately. As plants begin to exhibit rapid growth, water thoroughly, then allow the mix to dry until it is just slightly damp before watering again. You will get excellent results with a weekly application of a water soluble fertilizer at half strength.

Germination

Plumeria seeds germinate quite rapidly, pushing vigorously through the soil, often within three days and usually not more than a week or ten days. We always allow at least two weeks to be sure that all the slow starters have had a chance to emerge. The percentage of germination should be very high, usually not less than 70% and up to 100% for select seeds.

As the seedling emerges from the soil the sheath will be attached. As growth progresses, the developing plant will vigorously throw off this tough, fibrous membrane to reveal the cotyledons or "seed leaves". If the seedling should not be strong enough to push off the sheath you can help by moistening it and gently peeling it off. If not removed the seedling will turn brown and die. Although we never had to remove a sheath in the tropics where seedlings easily thrust off their encasement, we have encountered the problem here in Houston.

Pros and Cons of Propagating from Seed

In summary, there are several advantages and disadvantages in propagating plumerias from seed. First, the plus side! Seeds are easily handled and a large number of plants can be started in a small space with relatively little expense. Most important is the fact that all new cultivars must be produced from seed. Plumeria seedlings have more variability that any plant we know. Plant twenty seeds from the same pod and you are likely to get twenty different combinations of color, size and form, some resembling the female parent, others exhibiting totally different characteristics. If you have collected seeds from a superior parent with a number of desirable qualities such as size, color, shape, fragrance, and substance, you have an excellent chance of producing a hybrid of merit.

Dr. James L. Brewbaker, Professor of Horticulture and Genetics at the University of Hawaii at Manoa, was very helpful in building the plumeria collection at the Matrimandir Gardens by sending seeds from outstanding cultivars in Dr. Criley's plumeria collection. Dr. Criley later wrote: "The seeds I provided you were labelled with the name of the seed parent. That is all I can tell you about their origin, except that most of the parents are *P. acuminata*. From observations of the breeders lines, I would say you could expect quite a bit of variation, but most progeny will reflect the primary colors of the parents—the pinks and whites tend to predominate."

A note on seedlings from the 1980 issue of The Planter, in an article by M. Ratnasabapathy of the University of Malaya and J. Mossel of the Netherlands, is worth mentioning: "But, as pointed out by Stone (1970), the tap-root system of plants raised from seeds would confer an important advantage over propagation by cuttings."

What then are the negatives to growing plants from seed? From thousands of seeds of unknown origin one would be very fortunate to get more than a few cultivars superior to any of the named varieties available today. Almost all seeds available today are from unknown parentage. Many will be from inferior stock and the results may be disappointing. Also, for those interested in immediate gratification, the 3 to 4 year wait for flowers may be discouraging. Yet, the field is still wide open, the possibilities are unlimited and new cultivars are sure to emerge surpassing all we have seen to date.

From Seed to Flower

The timetable given by most of the expert plumeria growers we have met is usually 3 to 4 years. Given the long growing season we were fortunate to have in India (365 days to be exact!), we had phenomenal results with our seedlings. Most flowered in less than 2 years and we had one seedling from Hawaii flower in just over 10 months!

The conclusion: Give seedlings plenty of light and heat throughout the year; grow them under lights in winter, if possible; plant in organically rich, well-drained soil; feed and water generously during the growing season. Providing these conditions could reduce the waiting time as much as 40%.

An Additional Note on Seedlings

When a seed germinates, the first leaf-like appendages it produces are the cotyledons or "seed leaves". These are not true leaves, and in most cases do not resemble them, but are food storage organs that nourish the plant in its initial stage of growth. The best time to transplant is when the seedling has 2 or 3 sets of true leaves. Since plumeria seedlings grow at a fast pace it is best to transplant immediately into a 6 or 7 inch pot.

Cuttings

This is the easiest way to propagate plumerias and the fastest way to have plants in bloom. Even though propagation by cuttings is relatively foolproof, there are important considerations both in taking cuttings and in rooting them. Cuttings should only be taken from mature wood that is firm and grey in color. Immature cuttings of green wood are extremely difficult to root and are not recommended for the beginner. The ideal time to root cuttings is in late spring when soil temperature as well as air temperature has warmed sufficiently. With the techniques listed below, we have been able to successfully extend the rooting period from early spring through late summer with the same degree of success.

Type and Size of Cuttings

Tip cuttings 12 to 15 inches long with a diameter of ¾ to 1 inch are ideal. Stem cuttings (see Appendix A) have an open cut on the top and are susceptible to rot from rain or watering. Tip cuttings (literally, the tips of the branches), can be taken at any length desired as long as they include 3 to 4 inches of grey wood. Well-branched cuttings as large as 6 feet in length are easily rooted following the basic principles listed in this chapter.

Preparing the Cutting

After making a cutting, take the following steps:

Remove all large leaves in order to reduce transpiration and allow the energy to go into root formation. After the leaves are removed the latex will dry quickly and seal the tip. We have seen several cultivars that have such strength that their leaves and inflorescences may be left on while the cutting is rooting but this is recommended only for the experienced grower. In general it is best to remove all or most of the leaves and not allow the cutting to flower. (Many cuttings have a latent inflorescence that will emerge after the cutting is taken from the parent plant.)

If the base of a cutting has any jagged edges it is best to cut it cleanly. Cutting the base at a 45 degree angle will provide somewhat more surface area for callus formation, but the most critical point to remember is to allow the base of the cutting to dry thoroughly, at least 3 to 5 days (some growers recommend 2 to 3 weeks!). Drying should take place in a warm, shaded area protected from rain and moisture.

Types of Rooting Media

In more than twenty years of propagating plumerias from cuttings, we have experimented with a multitude of media and have had varying degrees of success. Our only failure (almost total) was with a predominantly vermiculite-based planting mix that held too much water. We would also caution against using soil since water retention is too great and the medium is not sterile or sufficiently porous to allow easy penetration of roots. Early experiments were with coarse sand gathered from the upper areas of beaches where the rain had leached away the salt over a period of years. Sand worked very well since there was no resistance to root formation but there were two drawbacks due to its weight. Not only were the pots very heavy to lift, but in trying to remove the cuttings when rooted, the tender, young roots would break off. Newly formed plumeria roots are extremely brittle and will snap off at the slightest disturbance. It is interesting to note that a friend in Hawaii, Jim Little, finds that beach sand, even with salt in it, is still one of the best mediums for rooting plumerias. As to the question of roots breaking due to the heaviness of sand, we were helped by another friend, James D. Jones, Jr., of Dallas, Texas. (This would apply only to a few cuttings planted in a container where the overall weight was not too much to lift.) James writes ". . . a very simple solution . . . which works very effectively for anything rooted in sand. Take a container of warm water, submerge the rooted cutting in its pot, gently lift cutting out. The water allows the roots to be released without damage."

Experiments in India were with coir dust, the peat-like residue from the coconut husk. We found it to be an ideal replacement for peat with almost identical moisture-holding characteristics as well as the soft fibrous quality so unique to peat moss. Coir dust, or "coconut peat" as I termed it, is a lightweight medium, easily handled, and loose enough for roots to form rapidly without resistance. We could dig down into the medium with our fingers and come up with a ball of roots every time.

Our success with coir dust in India led us to try peat moss here in Houston. Although this may seem hard to believe, Houston has a much cooler climate than South India, even in the summer! Since peat moss holds nearly 600 times its weight in water, we found the moisture retention was too great for plumerias. We then began blending coarse perlite with the peat and this worked very well. Still, it is easy to over-water so we cut back the peat even more. Our recommendation is ⅔ coarse perlite and ⅓ peat. The moisture-holding capacity is excellent, drainage is rapid, and cuttings don't rot even if one should be too generous occasionally with water. Although perlite is toxic to some plants, it has no adverse effects on plumerias. In fact, cuttings rooted in 100% perlite will develop a mass of roots. The bottom line is to achieve a lightweight medium that combines excellent air porosity and optimum drainage while holding just the right amount of moisture, is sterile, and has a texture that allows plumeria roots to penetrate with little resistance and form a mass adhering to the medium.

Rooting Cuttings in Water?

Yes, after all you have just read, the uniqueness of plumerias is such that many people have written that they have successfully rooted cuttings in water! Since we have not personally tried this we will quote directly from friends who have. Phil Brodhag writes: "Our son had a cutting in a glass of water that has been there for about two years. It has rooted well and is now planted." Barbara Anderson of Houston has also written: "You may include my experience with rooting plumerias in water in your handbook. Just stress the importance of letting the cutting dry 24 hours or the cutting will rot. I have put cuttings in water in November and December after the leaves have fallen off and the cutting will put leaves on without roots. Then in the springtime I pot them or put them in flower beds." Finally, a very interesting note from George Slusser, a dedicated grower in Washington: "The water-rooted cutting of Plumeria came from a packaged item, purchased either at a commercial greenhouse or from a novelty store in Honolulu, Hawaii. I placed it in a clear glass jar and put it in a west window, over the kitchen sink. There was about an inch to 1½ inches of water. I used a rooting powder. . . . I had no idea that water-rooting was novel for Plumeria. . . ." (Note: George has since conducted many successful experiments rooting plumerias in water. We have included some of his excellent photographs demonstrating the results.)

With plumerias we have found that exceptions are sometimes as valid as rules!

Planting the Cutting

When planting a cutting remember, as with seeds, to pre-moisten the medium. We have found that pressing down on the medium and packing it tightly both before and after inserting the cutting leads to faster root development. It is best not to plant cuttings too deep in order to reduce the possibility of rot. Plumerias will not produce roots from the sides of a cutting no matter how deep it is planted since all rooting takes place around the base. We prefer the simple method of filling a container with 4 to 5 inches of mix and inserting the cutting at an angle. Some growers allow the container to support the cuttings but we find with good compaction of the medium they will hold on their own. Many cuttings may be started in the same container but do not place them too close together as this will cut down on air circulation and lead to potential problems such as fungus.

This year we found the best container yet; molded plastic baskets (available everywhere) that are similar to laundry baskets but slightly smaller. We used a 16 x 21 x 10 inch basket, but there are many sizes available. The baskets are solid on the bottom and have open slits in the sides. We drilled several ¾ to 1 inch holes in the bottom, in the center and at the four corners to guarantee excellent drainage. We also placed a 5 or 6 inch strip of inexpensive ground cover cloth around the inside to prevent the medium from spilling out through the slits in the sides. We packed in about 5 inches of mix, pressing it firmly against the sides to hold the cloth in place. The two things we like most about the baskets are that they are lightweight and easily handled, and they allow plenty of air to circulate around the cuttings.

Before planting a cutting, first make a hole in the medium with a round dowel or stick approximately the same size as the cutting. Moisten the base of the cutting, shake off the excess moisture, then dip the cutting in a rooting hormone and shake off the excess powder. After many years of trials we are convinced of the effectiveness of rooting hormones, especially on the more difficult-to-root varieties. There are many types of rooting hormones available depending on the nature of the plant material one wishes to propagate. Our recommendation is to use a rooting hormone containing fungicide. For the most challenging varieties one may use a higher strength formulation available from growers supply houses.

In 1984 I made an initial experiment in the use of bottom heat by placing cuttings in one gallon plastic pots set in saucers on top of our gas water heater. It was not really a controlled experiment since most of the time I forgot to water! Yet, all of the cuttings came through in good health and were the first to root when I put them outside in the spring. This past year I repeated the experiment with some cuttings of rare species. I remembered to water and to my delight the cuttings were well-rooted before spring. In addition to being rare, these were also difficult species to root. This spring we had great success rooting some especially challenging varieties by using a propagation mat with a thermostat that kept the soil temperature at a constant 80 degrees.

The Rooting Process

The first stage of the rooting process is the formation of callus tissue at the base of the cutting. Because of the strong life-force in a plumeria cutting, callus tissue can often be seen forming at the base of cuttings that have been left out to dry for as long as 2 to 3 weeks after being removed from the parent plant. Callus tissue is white to creamy-white, almost translucent, and builds up around the base of a cutting. The tissue will often emerge only at one part of the base, at other times it will encircle it. Brittle white roots will emerge soon after the development of this tissue. Cuttings should not be disturbed during the rooting period in order to prevent shock and damage to new roots. Once started, roots develop quickly and densely and will become less brittle as they mature.

Watering Cuttings

With the new rooting mix formula we have developed there is much less chance of cuttings rotting due to overwatering. Watering once a week throughout most of the rooting period should be sufficient unless you are certain the medium has become dry throughout. Since the water retention of different mixes will vary considerably, it is best to develop a "feel" for the amount of water required. You can begin by testing with your finger, digging as deeply into the container as possible to feel whether the medium is wet, damp or dry. This takes some experience but stay with it and you'll develop the touch! If you feel insecure, a water meter with at least a 6 to 8 inch probe will be the best way to ascertain the proper moisture content. Ideally, the rooting medium should be damp but not wet, except when you water, and then you should soak the medium thoroughly. An exception would be the difficult-to-root cultivars, especially some of the red shades, which should be kept a bit on the dry side. On a scale of 1 to 10, with 1 being completely dry and 10 saturated, we would recommend keeping the moisture content between 5 and 6 for most cuttings and between 4 and 5 for the more challenging varieties. Moisture meters are calibrated in the same way.

Sun/Shade Requirements for Rooting Cuttings

Since we first published our handbook in 1985, we have conducted numerous experiments in light requirements for rooting cuttings. This spring we started cuttings in full sun, filtered light and under clear fiberglass. We found no appreciable difference in any of the exposures. We recently started cuttings in August under the same conditions (plus 95 degree heat and high humidity) with equal success. The only thing we would caution against is starting cuttings in dense shade where they would be more susceptible to rot through overwatering. Some growers start cuttings in the shade for a week or two and then move them into full sun.

Testing for Roots and Removing Rooted Cuttings

The next obvious question is how to know when the roots have formed sufficiently for transplanting. This can be a frustrating experience. Such is the energy in the stem of a plumeria that cuttings will often produce leaves and infloresences, exhibiting signs of vigorous growth, without even beginning to root. There is no harm in giving the cutting a very gentle tug to detect if there is resistance. Be careful, however, because a strong tug will rip off the brittle new roots. If you have any qualms about this it is best to insert your fingers down as far as possible into the medium, an inch or two from the stem of the cutting, and then pry upwards. If a root system has developed you can easily feel it and remove a "ball" with a minimum loss of roots. (Although it is admittedly hard on the fingernails, no trowel has the sensitivity of your hands!) On occasion some cuttings will show no signs of rooting or leaf growth. It is best to remove these and examine for rot at the base. If the cutting has begun to rot you can cut it back completely to green wood where no sign of brown remains, then allow it to dry thoroughly and start the rooting process over again.

Air-layering

Air-layering involves more work than propagation by cuttings or seeds, but it is the surest method since the part to be rooted is not separated from the parent plant until roots have formed. One may wish to try this on rare varieties.

As with cuttings, it is preferable to make air-layerings when the plant is in an active stage of growth. It does not matter whether the branch you have chosen is flowering or not. The best time for air-layering would be from a week or two after the plant has resumed normal growth in the spring until a month before the end of summer.

Be sure the branch is mature and at least 1 inch in diameter. It is best to have 12 to 18 inches of growth beyond the point where you want the roots to form. At that point, make two separate cuts encircling the branch, about 1½ inches apart (see Appendix A). Scrape away all of the cambium layer down to hard wood so the cut cannot heal over. Then pack a ball of moist sphagnum moss or peat moss around the cut and cover with plastic wrap or a piece of plastic bag, tying both the top and bottom securely with string or twist-ties. It will take from 1½ to 3 months for roots to fully develop but you will be able to see them growing through the moss. If you have wrapped the plastic tightly, you will probably not have to water the moss again.

When the roots are well-formed, cut the branch off just below the root formation, remove the plastic carefully and plant the rooted layering with the moss in a 10 or 12 inch container.

Grafting

Our first experiments with grafting were both memorable and surprisingly successful. Once again, our class of school children in Auroville participated in the experiment. (If we succeeded with six year olds holding and wrapping electrical tape and nine and ten year olds making the incisions to join stock and scion, I think everyone who is interested should give it a try!) One week our goal was to create a "Rainbow Tree" by grafting scions of different plumeria cultivars onto a semi-dwarf variety of *Plumeria obtusa.* We used standard grafting techniques, mainly the "whip and tongue" method, and the wedge or V-shaped graft, making certain that stock and scion were about the same diameter, then wrapped the entire area with electrical tape. To further protect the grafts from breaking we splinted the grafted area with bamboo sticks.

For the grafting experiment we used mature wood about 12 inches in length and about 1 inch thick, taking care to be sure that the cambium layers on stock and scion were in good contact. Four to six weeks later we removed the tape to find the grafts perfectly joined. Since we did the grafting in early spring we were able to enjoy a profusion of color on our "Rainbow Tree" the same year!

Maui Beauty

White Shell

FAMILY MEMBERS

Mandevilla x amabilis
'Alice duPont'

Mandevilla boliviensis
White Dipladenia

Urichites lutea
Yellow Mandevilla

Allmanda Williamsii
'Stansill's Double'

Mandevilla sanderi
'Red Riding Hood'

Mandevilla sanderi
'Rosea'

Thevetia peruviana
Yellow Oleander

Allamanda cathartica
Var. 'Hendersonii'

Adenium obesum
Desert Rose

FAMILY MEMBERS

Catharanthus roseus
Madagascar
Periwinkle

Tabernaemontana
divaricata
Crepe Jasmine

Nerium oleander
'Mrs. George
Roeding'

Carissa grandiflora
'Compacta'

Allamanda cathartica
'Cherries Jubilee'

Nerium oleander
'Mathilde Ferrier'

Trachelospermum
jasminoides
Star Jasmine

Nerium oleander
'Martha Hanna
Hensley'

Petite Pink, also known in Hawaii as Dwarf Pink Singapore.

SOILS AND SOIL MIXES

Soil Mixes for Containers

Plumerias are very heavy feeders and respond best to rich, well-drained, organic soil mixes and frequent supplemental fertilizing. Whether potting or repotting, the following is an excellent formula from an expert Indian gardener, Sri Parichand, with whom we had the honor to work for many years. His 'Singapore' plumerias were the most beautifully grown pot plants we have ever seen; they were compact, usually 2 to 3 feet in height and about the same spread; the foliage a glossy, dark green, covered with intensely fragrant, pure white flowers month after month from April through October. Here is his formula:

> 50% well-rotted cow manure
> 25% leaf mold
> 25% good garden soil
> 1 handful bone meal per 12 inch pot

There are many good packaged soils and soilless products available in the U.S. We prefer an organic-based planting mix that has a high percentage of compost. In addition to bone meal, there are numerous organic ingredients that may be added to a basic soil mix such as composted manures, blood meal, rock phosphate, perlite, vermiculite, peat moss and charcoal. All have their value for certain plants but we do not recommend the addition of peat moss or vermiculite for plumerias as these tend to hold too much moisture. The planting medium must be well-drained and well-aerated.

Ingredients that are too fine will settle in time and create an oxygen depleted zone toward the bottom half of the pot and roots will not be able to grow past that point. Water stagnation and ultimately root-rot may follow. Plants have many ways of telling us they are in soil that is too heavy or poorly drained. Usually one will first see drooping leaves (not due to dryness but rather to oversaturation), or soft stems, and if one pulls the plant out of the container there will be root-rot or no root development at all.

To sum up the ideal soil mix: first, it must be rich in organic nutrients and exceptionally well-drained, yet have excellent moisture-holding capacity, with well distributed particle size throughout to avoid fines settling towards the bottom and inhibiting further root growth; finally, a good container mix will be easy to wet and have a wealth of beneficial microorganisms present to assure a slow and balanced release of nutrients.

Soil Preparation for Planting in the Ground

Planting directly in the ground is a bit less challenging than container culture but there are still a number of specifics that need to be addressed. Although plumerias will tolerate many apparently adverse conditions, they will not survive in heavy soils that tend to become waterlogged. Few soils are naturally ideal with a basic composition of well-drained, friable sandy loam possessing the following characteristics: excellent drainage combined with optimum moisture-holding capacity, substantial organic content, high microorganism activity, adequate NPK and trace elements in the right balance to assure sustained, vigorous and healthy plant performance. Soil pH, unless extremely unbalanced, is not very critical to plumerias since they will do well in pH ranges from neutral to slightly acid to slightly alkaline. In fact, they are very tolerant of many conditions in nature. In Botany of the Maya Area, Miscellaneous Papers XIV-XXI, published in 1940, there is an account of an expedition that collected specimens of *Plumeria rubra* from limestone hills bordering the Mountain Pine Ridge in the Yucatan Peninsula. For container planting we prefer to begin with a soil mix that is slightly acid since watering, especially with treated water, tends to raise the pH.

PLANTING AND TRANSPLANTING

Transplanting Seedlings and Rooted Cuttings

General rules of horticulture apply to plumerias as to any other plant. In transplanting, the main objectives are to disturb the root system as little as possible and not let the roots dry out from exposure to wind or sun. Even though plumerias are tougher than many plants, you should still follow these basic steps:

1. Have everything in readiness before removing a cutting or seedling from its container. This includes wetting the soil in the seedling or cutting pot as well as the soil in the new container. Have additional soil ready for topping up as well as plant stakes and ties.
2. It is best to transplant towards the end of the afternoon, after the heat of the day has passed. The plant will then have the cooler hours of the evening and early morning to recover from the shock of transplanting. Work rapidly, in the shade and out of the wind, allowing the least amount of time to elapse between removing the plant from the rooting medium and placing it in the new soil mix. This will insure that the roots have minimum exposure to the air.
3. Always try to remove the new plant with a good "ball" of soil around the roots, taking special care to break as few roots as possible.
4. Center the plant in the container about 1½ inches below the rim and gently firm the soil on all sides. Remember to cover plumeria cuttings only just above the depth at which the roots begin. You can get away with planting slightly deeper but we have had problems on occasion with stem rot during winter storage. Since plumerias will root quickly in their new container, staking is only temporary.
5. Lastly, water thoroughly using a transplant vitamin containing Vit. B1 (Superthrive, root stimulator, etc.) to reduce shock and stimulate new growth.

Repotting Container Grown Plumerias

It is easy to repot well-established plumerias in containers, especially if one has a strong back! Actually, it is much easier to repot mature plants than rooted cuttings or seedlings. As your plumerias grow, their root systems become stronger and can form a dense mass in just one season. The brittleness disappears and individual roots become tough and stringy. Often they will protrude through the drainage holes in the container. This is a sure sign that you should repot. Aesthetic proportions are a second consideration. One should achieve a harmonious ratio of plant to container size. A top heavy plant in a small container has no balance (aesthetic or physical), and a small plant in a large container looks just as awkward.

The same transplanting rules given above apply to repotting, though the actual process differs somewhat. First, remove the plant from the original container. This may involve cutting some of the roots that have pushed through the drainage holes. When the roots have grown too large to get them back through the holes without tearing and scraping, cut them cleanly off at the edge of the pot. It is better to have the root ball slightly on the dry side rather than moist, the object being to remove the plant without breaking up the root ball. Lift the plant by the trunk, hold the container a few inches above the ground and tap the container with the hand (or trowel or piece of wood). The container should fall to the ground, the plant safely removed. A second method, for plants that are not too tall, is to lift the plant, turn it upside down and tap the edge of the container on any solid edge such as a wheelbarrow, workbench, etc. This should loosen the ball and the container can then be lifted off. This is a good method for transplanting from container to ground or for gently handling plants with weak root balls, for after removing the container one can place both hands under the ball and lower it to an upright position. The plant can then be placed in the ground or a larger container.

On removing your plumeria from its pot, check to see if the roots are encircling each other. This is a common occurance in plants grown in containers. Once this begins it is rather like a bad habit—very difficult to break! In fact, all pot bound plants will behave in the same way and their roots will not change this circular pattern even if planted in a large hole with an ideal medium. Do not hesitate to "comb" the roots downward so they are once again in a vertical position where they can spread out into the earth. It is best to cut off the encircling roots from the bottom of the root ball with a sharp knife, or pruners. Established plumerias regenerate roots rapidly and, instead of suffering a set-back, they will be invigorated by the treatment.

Top-dressing and Root Pruning

Rather than repotting plants the second year it is easier to top-dress. This technique produces amazing results in growth and flowering with a minimum of labor. The method has been utilized in the tropics for hundreds of years, where sun and heat rapidly deplete nutrients in containers.

Remove as much soil as possible from the top of the container without damaging the roots. You will find that you can remove a fair amount of soil from a two year old plant. After removing the soil sprinkle 1 handful of bone meal around the exposed roots and cover to the original level with a mixture of 3 parts well-rotted cow manure and 1 part sandy loam. Top dressing is most effective when done during the first warm days of spring.

Another method is to root prune your plants and replace them in the same size container. With the ball on the dry side for easier removal, follow the methods listed above for repotting, then cut away about 1 inch on each side of the root ball and from

1 to 2 inches from the bottom. Have your container mix ready and, following all the above directions for preparing containers, fill with the new medium plus a handful of bone meal, pack the soil tightly against the roots for good contact and water thoroughly.

Root pruning is best done during the spring when new roots will regenerate rapidly but it may also be done in the fall when removing plants from containers for winter storage.

Plumerias respond very well to root pruning as it is a stimulus to new growth and flowering. The technique may also help recalcitrant plants to bloom, especially if transplanted into a larger container with organically rich soil.

After transplanting, always water with a transplant vitamin and place the plant in filtered light or light shade.

SUN/SHADE REQUIREMENTS

Although there are a number of factors that will influence the amount of sun we give our plumerias, the most important thing to remember is that in nature, plumerias grow in full sun exposures and are not found anywhere in heavy shade. We have observed plumerias under all types of sun/shade conditions and have found that unless they have an absolute minimum of one half day exposure to full sun, they will not bloom. We once planted some varieties of *Plumeria obtusa* along a fence line where faster growing trees eventually shaded them too heavily and the results were remarkable. Flowering diminished rapidly, limbs became weak and leggy stretching for sunlight, and finally the plants stopped flowering altogether. As a general rule the more sun one gives, the better the flowering one can expect. There are, however, exceptions; some cultivars will not tolerate the most intense afternoon sun and should be allowed to have partial afternoon shade or filtered light. Also, in areas of high air pollution, leaf burn often occurs with plumerias in full sun and plants grown in containers seem to be more sensitive than those in the ground. It may be necessary to give your plants full morning sun exposure and filtered light from about 2:00 pm. Plumerias planted in containers, especially in the southern states where the problem is more likely to occur, can be moved about until the best location is found for a particular variety.

WATERING

Watering Plumerias in Containers

Watering is a skill—or perhaps an intuition—developed over the years through an intimate contact with plants that enables one to understand their widely divergent needs. Weather conditions (sun, overcast skies, wind), time of the year, size of plants, size of root mass, size and type of container, and type of growing medium are all factors that will determine the amount and frequency of water necessary. Fortunately, plumerias are very resilient and a missed watering will not send them into shock. A general rule for most plants is to water thoroughly and infrequently rather than shallowly at brief intervals.

Water plumerias thoroughly when the soil is dry and then allow the medium to dry out before watering again. Normally containers larger than 2 gal. need water only once a week unless temperatures are in the 90's or humidity is unusually low when they may need to be watered as often as twice a week. During periods of intense heat and drought one may have to water every other day but more than this is not necessary. Smaller containers and recently transplanted rooted cuttings or seedlings will need more frequent watering and should be monitored on a day to day basis. All plants tell us rather quickly when they are in need of water, first with flaccid leaves, then overall wilting. You will be amazed at how tolerant plumerias are, however, for they can survive neglect and absolute minimum care better than most plants.

Watering Plumerias in the Ground

Our experiences in India taught us that plumerias planted in the ground require very little water. During the long hot summers we watered mature trees only once a month, filling the 3 to 4 foot berm around the plant. Newly established trees and younger plants were watered weekly. Experiments conducted in Green Belt areas surrounding the township of Auroville determined that newly established plantings of plumerias would not survive months of drought without supplemental water. It was also found that overly generous waterings in our nursery plantings caused excessively rapid growth that developed weak and spindly limbs, easily susceptible to breaking. Overwatering promotes heavy vegetative growth and most plumeria growers would prefer flowers. If you plant plumerias in the ground, water sparingly.

FERTILIZING

Plumeria growers have discovered many different techniques that work for them. We have utilized a number of these along with some of our own tried and true methods and have come to the age-old conclusion that you should continue with whatever has been successful for you, even if the "experts" are not inclined to agree. "If it ain't broke, don't fix it", applies as much to plants as anything else!

There are, however, certain nutrient combinations and fertilizing principles that almost always produce the desired results. Plumerias thrive best with a fertilizer low in nitrogen and high in phosphorous, with ample potash and balanced trace elements, especially iron and magnesium, which help prevent chlorosis and leaf burn, respectively. Nitrogen is necessary to promote overall plant development including healthy stems and foliage, but too much nitrogen will promote vegetative growth at the expense of flowering. NPK is the chemical abbreviation for nitrogen (N), phosphorus (P), and potash (K). By law, all fertilizers must be labelled with the percentages of NPK in their formulation. Nitrogen is available in many forms, either as a quick release or a slow-release nutrient. Phosphorus is available in quick release form as superphosphate and triple-superphosphate as well as in water-soluble forms. Both rock phosphate and bone meal are excellent organic, slow-acting, long-lasting sources of phosphorous. Composted manures are valuable slow-release nitrogen sources but must be fully composted to prevent burning. Compost and leaf mold are the most valuable soil amendments for providing a slow-release, natural source of nutrients and microorganisms.

Readily available in the U.S. and elsewhere are excellent formulations of water soluble fertilizers with high phosphorus content. These fertilizers are faster acting, being immediately available to the plant, and may be applied to the soil or as a foliar feed. Water soluble, chelated trace elements (minerals) are most useful in correcting minor nutrient deficiencies.

When using granular fertilizers it is best to water plants thoroughly before applying the fertiizer and then water again lightly to insure that the fertilizer is moved down into the medium where it can be utilized by the roots.

Fish emulsion and other organic plant foods, whether derived from sludge, seaweed, earthworm castings, guano, etc. will benefit your plants tremendously if used sparingly on a regular basis. Magnesium sulfate (Epsom salts), helps the greening process and lowers soil pH, as azalea growers have long known. Magnesium is the central core of the chlorophyll molecule and is a resonator for the photosynthetic process. Magnesium sulfate will help prevent leaf scorch and, if used as a foliar feed, will be faster acting and more effective than iron.

Controlled-release or time-release fertilizers are beneficial in providing sustained release of nutrients over a given time frame, but most are balanced formulations such as 13-13-13, or high nitrogen blends such as 18-6-12, and are therefore not recommended for plumerias.

In tropical areas where manures and oil cake residues are easily available and very inexpensive, gardeners often make manure "teas" and oilcake paste. A weekly application of groundnut (peanut) oil cake made into a paste and spread evenly over the top of the pot then watered in, will promote larger flowers and more abundant inflorescences. To make oil cake paste, soak an equal amount of oil cake and water for six hours. This will render a thin paste and soaking for six hours will not produce a bad odor. Manure "tea" is made by soaking one part manure in three parts water and then straining off the liquid, diluting it to a desired strength and applying it to the plant and watering lightly.

With all fertilizers, a good general rule to follow is to apply light applications of fertilizer frequently rather than heavy doses at longer intervals. We learned a secret from orchid growers in Thailand that has enabled them to double and triple their cut-flower production. Instead of fertilizing with a tablespoon of fertilizer per gallon every two weeks, they dilute the amount to 1/14 and fertilize every day. Their procedure is to fertilize in the morning and then water in the afternoon. This washes off any salts that may accumulate on the plant while the fertilizer has already been absorbed!

After studying the nutritional requirements for plumerias for 20 years, we have recently formulated a fertilizer that meets all their needs, whether in containers or in the ground. This is a supplemental fertilizer in granular form that should be applied every 7 to 10 days, from the beginning of the growing season in spring until 1 or 2 months before the first frost date. It contains many of the ingredients listed in this chapter in the ratios we have found to be most beneficial.

There seem to be two entirely opposite experiences in growing plumerias in containers that should be noted. Some growers insist that their plants will not bloom until they are completely rootbound. Others are certain that plumerias do not like to be rootbound and must be potted in larger containers or removed from their containers each year to have their roots trimmed and then repotted. After examining the evidence on both sides, we offer the suggestion that perhaps the question is not so much whether the plants are rootbound or not, but how much nutrition is being supplied.

Proper fertilizing is the key to successful flowering. Be generous in feeding your plumerias, feed them regularly and experiment with top-dressing if you cannot or do not wish to root prune your plants. The more care you take in feeding, the greater the rewards in flower production and overall vigor.

MULCHING

The importance of mulching cannot be overemphasized. The many benefits to be derived from proper mulching include: moderating soil temperatures, weed suppression, moisture retention, the building up of organic matter and aesthetic enhancement. When mulch is properly applied it will even inhibit the spread of soil-borne diseases by preventing soil from splashing onto the leaves. If you plant in the ground, by all means mulch. Even if you garden only in containers, mulching will help prevent excessive evaporation and heat stress by providing an insulating blanket between sensitive feeder roots and the sun's rays.

PRUNING

Plumerias rarely need pruning since they have basically symmetrical growth without problems of crossing branches or dead limbs. Still, there are valid reasons for pruning. Many plumerias, especially seedlings, will produce rapid vertical growth without a balance of horizontal growth, bearing their flowers at too great a height to be appreciated and creating problems of unwieldiness when the time comes for winter storage.

There are no great secrets to pruning plumerias. They can be safely cut at any time of the year as the drying latex will heal the wound quickly. Be sure to cut just above a node and at a slight angle. Plumeria nodes are fairly close together so this should not present a problem. At least one and as many as three or more branches will emerge from the latent buds beneath the cut. Observing the direction of the bud will enable you to control the direction of the terminal and lateral branches. Some sources recommend treating the cuts with asphalt tree paint. In areas of frequent rainfall this may have some validity but we have always found healing to be so rapid that this treatment is unnecessary.

Do not hesitate to prune to create better branched plants that will produce flowers at a desired height. Plumerias will branch rapidly after pruning and in tropical areas will even resume flowering in a few months. Dave Emison, of Houston, has shared some of his experiences in pruning *Plumeria obtusa* with us. Dave was hesitant to prune his plants and like other devoted plumeria growers found it to be a traumatic (for him, not the plant!) experience at first. But when his 'Singapores' grew too tall and became unmanageable, Dave finally resorted to pruning. His purpose was to create denser, more compact plants, to reduce height so the flowers could be viewed more comfortably and to enable the plants to be handled more easily. Dave envisioned the best place to make a cut so that the resulting growth would fill in the plant most aesthetically. On 'Singapore', he usually had three branches form immediately beneath the cut. His plants responded very well and once pruned and structured as Dave wished, he found that most didn't require any severe pruning for at least another three to four years.

One note of caution should be added, however, in pruning plumerias. Remember that plumerias produce flowers from the tips of their branches. In areas with shorter growing seasons than in the tropics, a plant may not have time to develop an inflorescence until the year following the pruning. Also, pruning sometimes causes branches to form at unattractive angles to the main stem. By contrast, branches that are produced at the base of a bloom stalk are always pleasing and symmetrical. You will achieve better results by fertilizing and getting plants to branch as a result of blooming.

HYBRIDIZING

There comes a time when having successfully grown and flowered plumerias from cuttings and seeds, both in containers and in the ground; having learned the best soil mixes and fertilization schedules; and having achieved the upper hand with insects and diseases, the plumeria enthusiast turns his or her attention to hybridizing. What if, one says, I could combine this deep red with that prolific, large-flowered white and achieve the best qualities of each? Thus begins, for many, a direction that will become a lifelong preoccupation, attempting to create more and more beautiful, long-lasting and fragrant flowers, aspiring towards perfection.

Let's look briefly at some of the most desirable traits of plumerias and the qualities we would like to develop. Here are some ideas; not necessarily in order of importance:

1. Flower substance — Improved substance would enhance the keeping quality of a flower—and who would not like to have a flower that would last many days in perfect condition? Too many of today's seedlings have petals that are thin, easily bruised and fade quickly.

2. Intensity of fragrance — We have already distinguished 12 characteristic fragrances; from the scent of coconut oil to many types of citrus; from the smell of ripe peaches to the haunting, heady aroma of jasmine and the unforgettable Frangipani perfume. Through hybridizing we might intensify fragrances and

possibly create new ones, adding to the range of perfumes we already enjoy from the many plumerias in cultivation today.

3. Flower shape and size — This is another fascinating area for exploration and one to which Bill Moragne, in Hawaii, devoted much time. Could one create flowers 7 to 8 inches across with shapes like pinwheels or dinner plates? Why not? A number of cultivars already approach 6 inches and we have read reports of hybrids of similar size in other areas of the tropics. We have grown many that measured 4 to 5 inches and have many yet to introduce from other countries that could form the basis of breeding stock for the future.

4. Flower color — Endless possibilities abound for new colors and color combinations. This is an exciting field. We have seen some hybrids that border on lavender, some tending toward pure orange, and occasionally a few with variegations that are truly remarkable. We can see the extraordinary work achieved by plant breeders in other fields such as roses, gladiolus, annuals and perennials, and once we begin controlled breeding programs with plumerias, we will be amazed at the results.

5. Duration and prolificacy of bloom — Perhaps in the future we will be able to develop plants that will flower abundantly from the first warm weather until the onset of winter, extending our enjoyment immeasurably.

6. Size and density of inflorescences — Many inflorescences have sparse blooms or only open a few flowers at a time. Through selective breeding we might increase the size of the inflorescence, the number of flowers open at one time and the density of the flowers in a cluster.

7. Plant size and shape — Experiments are already under way at the University of Hawaii's Experimental Station at Waimanolo to produce compact plants with many breaks so that more flowers can be produced per plant for the lei industry. The more growing tips a plant produces, the more flower clusters it can bear. Lei growers are also looking for intensity of color and good substance so that leis will last longer. I'm sure that all of us in non-tropical areas would appreciate low, bushy plants ablaze with color during the growing season and easily handled for winter storage!

Menninger, in <u>Flowering Trees of the World</u>, can easily inspire us to begin hybridizing with the following quotes:

Most Plumeria blossoms are 3 to 3½ inches across, but large-flowered types have developed as distantly as Kenya and Hawaii. Jex-Blake (<u>Gardening in East Africa</u>, Ed.4 Longmans, Green & Co. London, 1957) tells of receiving seeds from a friend in Tanganyika who had a very good reddish-orange kind. It had hybridized with the common white, and nearly every plant that resulted produced flowers of different sizes, colors, and even slightly different scent. They varied in color from pink to white and lemon-yellow and were almost as large as magnolias.

William F. Whitman reports from Honolulu: "On a tree in the Manoa Valley, in a partially shaded location which received full sunlight in the later afternoon, the average size of the larger blooms was six inches across the individual flower."

Albert de LeStang in northern Queensland reported the basal tube crimson, underside of petals golden veined with rose, the edges in and out bright rose, the inside petal whitish tinged golden, the base canary yellow with red centre; all colors fade to pale white, gold and rose as the flower ages. At the flush flowering he considered this variety the loveliest of Plumerias.

We hope we have whetted your appetite enough to venture into the rewarding world of hybridizing. When we first published our <u>Handbook on Plumeria Culture</u> in 1985, we knew of no controlled hybridizing experiments anywhere in the world. Since then we have had the special privilege of meeting Mary Moragne Cook and learning of her father's success in hybridizing plumerias. We have devoted an entire chapter in this second edition to his unique work.

Pollination

Pollination in nature occurs by the action of insects, wind and water. For certain plants there are more propitious times of the day for pollination, when the pod parent is more receptive. Through experience we learn the best time to transfer the pollen from the pollen parent to the seed parent. (With hibiscus in India, we had our best results at about 10:00 a.m.)

The reproductive systems of plants are extremely diverse in form but will contain the following:

Female parts: Pistil — consisting of the stigma, style and ovary.

Male parts: Stamen — consisting of the anthers (recepticles for the pollen) and the filaments (that hold the anthers).

It is more difficult to pollinate plumerias than many other plants such as hibiscus and passion flowers which have reproductive parts that are generally large, visible and accessible. It is exacting work requiring good eyes and a steady hand but you will have all the necessary knowledge after reading this chapter. Even though some plumeria varieties do not bear seeds, all flowers contain both male and female reproductive parts. In the following description of the steps of pollination, we refer to the flower or plant from which the pollen is taken as the "male parent" or "pollen parent" and the flower or plant to which the pollen is transferred as the "female parent" or "seed parent". With "open pollination", only the seed parent is known. Even if we transfer pollen from a pollen parent of our choice, we cannot be certain that this will be the only pollen received by the female parent unless we have first emasculated the anthers from the female to avoid the possibility of self-pollination. The female flower must then be covered to be certain that no other pollen is transmitted by insects, etc. Despite the claim by some breeders that mixing pollen on the stigmas of the female parent can lead to wonderful color combinations in new hybrids, nature simply doesn't work this way. Even though pollen from several different male parents may be applied to a stigma, only the single grain whose tube reaches the embryo sac first will complete the pollination and all the others do not play a part in the fertilization process.

When we have chosen the seed parent, we must then gain access to the reproductive parts which are hidden deep near the base of the corolla tube. There are various methods of achieving this and we will examine some of them.

An excellent step-by-step description of how to hybridize plumerias is found in Circular 410, entitled Hawaiian Plumerias, by Watson, Chinn, Clay and Brewbaker, issued by the University of Hawaii Cooperative Extension Service (no longer in print):

1. Select in the morning two newly opened flowers, one as seed parent and one as pollen parent.

2. Cut off corolla tube about one-half inch above junction of the tube and the stem. Allow latex to flow from the cut and dry the latex with some absorbent material.

3. Carefully open the corolla tube with a sharp needle to expose the style and some of the surrounding anthers.

4. Remove the anthers to avoid possible self-pollination.

5. With a needle introduce the pollen to the mid-section of the style or within the receptive collar of sticky fluid.

6. Protect the style and reduce drying by slipping a 2-inch piece of large plastic drinking straw over the style and plugging it at the top with wet cotton.

7. Tag the pollinated flower, indicating the parents used — "Sherman (seed) x Rainbow (pollen)" — and the date.

A successful pollination will result in the fertilization of the ovaries, causing 2 seed pods to enlarge within 2 weeks after pollination. In about 7 months these seed pods will be nearly mature and should be covered with a paper bag to prevent the loss of the hybrid seed. The seed pod will split open in from about 8-8½ months from the date of pollination.

It will help to:
1. Use flowers on trees that are known to have set several seed pods natu-

rally. It is preferable that the trees be located where flower picking is controlled.

2. Sterilize pollen applicator with 95 per cent alcohol before pollinating with different pollen to avoid pollen contamination.

3. Label pollinated flowers with bright colored tags and secure them to the "stems" of flowers to record the pollination and to discourage accidental picking.

4. Allow seed pod to open naturally before harvesting seeds.

5. Harvest seeds promptly to protect them from being eaten by insects.

6. Try reversing parents if your first attempt is not successful, since some plumeria flowers are better for seed than for pollen parents.

With this as our starting point, we can consciously begin hybridizing plumerias, assisting Nature in her varied and splendid creations.

PESTS AND DISEASES, PROBLEMS AND SOLUTIONS

Plumerias are remarkably resistant to insects and diseases. In India we experienced no problems whatsoever and in 12 years we never had to spray! Occasionally during times of heavy rainfall, black fungus would appear briefly only to disappear with warm sunny days.

When any plant is introduced into an environment that is markedly different from its natural habitat it may be susceptible to problems not formerly encountered. In Houston we have seen a number of such instances. Plumerias grown in areas where there is insufficient air circulation are often attacked by spider mites. Spider mites can often be washed off with a strong jet of water and are also relatively easy to control with insecticidal soap. Some growers have had success with Malathion even though it is not listed as a specific control.

In Hawaii, we have seen large plantings of plumerias attacked by borers, the larvae of the long-horned beetle. Dr. Criley writes: "Short of spraying weekly and using very toxic chemicals to treat the trees, there is little that can be done." Dr. Criley also mentions that he must prune out dead branches every time he goes over to the trial grounds of the University of Hawaii at Waimanolo. We would like to emphasize that everyone on the mainland U.S. should pay very close attention to their plants and be ever watchful for borers. Plumeria cuttings are being sold in plastic bags at airports and gift shops in Hawaii by a growing number of different companies who may or may not be careful to take cuttings only from "clean" trees. In the early stages, borers can be detected by the presence of tiny, pin-sized holes in the bark from which exudes a small dot of black material. The area soon becomes soft as the borer eats away the inside of the stem. If you find evidence of a borer in a branch, cut the branch back to clean wood and destroy it.

In his letter of September 14, 1988, Dr. Criley responded to several of our questions as follows: "I asked our extension entomologists about the long-horned beetle, Lagocheirus obsoletus Thoms. There is no extensive published information about it in plumeria that they are aware of. The main mention I am aware of is in Univ. Hawaii Cooperative Extension Circular 410 (Watson, Chinn, Clay and Brewbaker, 1965). Even in this, there is not a straightforward recommendation for control, mentioning only malathion. I do recall one recommendation for the use of the insecticide SEVIN (carbaryl) which would control the insect if it chews on treated tissue and consumes the insecticide. I am not aware of specific recommendations and have done no studies on the problem. The entomologist indicated that it does attack other plants and mentioned having isolated it in some banyans here in Hawaii. Thus, I can't really say when it emerges and lays its eggs, how many instars (stages of development) there are and how long they take, etc. It would be interesting to try biological controls such as the new nematode biologicals which attack various insect grubs and caterpillars, but the main problem is to get them into contact with a grub that has embedded itself inside a branch. It might deserve support by PSA [Plumeria Society of America] to study controls if they would like to make such a grant."

In Circular 410 mentioned above (and quoted elsewhere in our handbook), the authors include a section on "Insects and Diseases" from which we quote two relevant paragraphs: "One insect which has recently caused considerable damage to limbs of old established trees is the grub of the long-horned beetle. These larvae are whitish or yellowish, soft-bodied, and possess powerful mouthparts for biting into the hardest of wood. Wilting of established limbs of the plumeria may indicated the presence of this insect under the bark. If the insects are not present in large numbers, remove the larva by cutting into the bark. Since weakened trees seem to be more prone to attack from these beetles, potential damage may be averted by maintaining the trees in a vigorous condition."

"If insect injury is serious, a regular spraying program may be necessary to maintain clean and healthy plants."

The authors recommend Malathion and Captan for borers. They also include the following observation: "In Hawaii, disease attributed to bacteria, fungi, and viruses are rarely serious on plumeria trees." They mention scale insects, beetles, and thrips as well as mites and aphids, all of which are not difficult to control with the use of insecticidal soap and/or a specifically approved chemical.

We have mentioned the incidence of sooty mold formation on limbs and trees. This is a black, powdery fungus that is unsightly and grows on the secretions from many of the above-mentioned insects. Again, it is easily controlled by an insecticidal soap or even soapy water applied with a forceful nozzle spray.

A fungus that attacks the growing tips of the plumeria can be quite serious if not controlled in the early stages. If not treated, not only will it destroy any emerging buds but will prevent any further development of the growing tips, eventually killing the plant. If a systemic fungicide (we have had excellent results with Benomyl), is applied directly to the infected area, the problem, which seems to occur with high humidity, is rapidly controlled. Bayleton has become available as a granular systemic just this year and should prove efficacious for most fungal problems when applied to the soil and watered in thoroughly.

In the past five years a "rust" fungus, *Coleosporium domingense*, which manifests as bright orange pustules on the undersurfaces of plumeria leaves, has appeared on plumerias in Houston gardens. In its initial stages it was easily controlled by Daconil 2787 (active ingredient chlorothalonil), but this was not effective on advanced cases. Mr. Larry W. Barnes, the Extension Plant Pathologist of the Texas A & M Agricultural Extension Service and Mr. Rayford G. Kay, Harris County Extension Agent (retired) examined and identified the rust in October, 1984. Their recommendation was Bayleton, a highly effective rust fungicide that is systemic. They wrote further that there was no fungicide currently cleared to be used for rust control on plumerias.

Since the above was written we have discovered an article in the <u>Proceedings of the Florida State Horticultural Society. 97:247-248, 1984</u>. The author, R.T. McMillan, Jr., has written an excellent article entitled: "Oxycarboxin a New Fungicide for Control of Frangipani Rust in Nursery and Field". Mr. McMillan's research concludes that ". . . foliar sprays of oxycarboxin at 1.2 g and 1.7 g per liter effectively controlled rust [Coleosporium dominguense (Burk.) Arth.] of frangipani (Plumeria rubra L.) in nursery and field trials. Oxycarboxin effectively stopped defoliation as well." In discussions with Howard Walters, Director of the Houston Rose Society, and from recent correspondence with Dr. Richard Criley, we have learned that oxycarboxin is the active ingredient of Plantvax and that it is a systemic fungicide effective in controlling rust. Howard says it is the best fungicide he has found for the control of rust on roses and grapes. Also, it is a low concentration material and safe for the user. One application will suffice for roses with no leaf damage. Plantvax-75W is readily available in the U.S. and is used extensively by rose growers in California.

We quote further from Mr. McMillan's research: "Oxycarboxin (Plantvax-75W) is a wettable powder suitable for use as a spray when suspended in water. . . . Frangipani rust is an annual problem for nurseries and home owners in South Florida and the Caribbean region. The disease reduces the saleability of nursery stock and the aesthetic beauty of a full foliage flowering plant. The use of oxycarboxin not only reduces the disease but has an obvious advantage over the other recommended fungicides [Dr. McMillan tested mancozeb, ferbam, and sulphur as well] since it only takes 4 applications as compared to 8 or more weekly sprays with presently used chemicals. Oxycarboxin as a soil drench might be [as] effective as the foliar sprays but such evaluation has not been made." Lastly, Dr. McMillan writes: "There were no toxic effects observed on the leaves, flowers or stems with oxycarboxin at the test rates and spray frequencies evaluated. At present oxycarboxin is approved by Environmental Protection Agency (EPA) for use on ornamentals and is available on the market."

When spraying for rust remember to treat the upper surface of the leaves where the fungus begins, as well as the lower surface.

Having grown thousands of seedlings, Elizabeth Thornton cautions against the fungus gnat whose invisible larvae feed on the tender new roots of plumeria seedlings. We quote her recommendations for control: "An application of 5% Sevin dust watered in or 5% liquid Sevin used every three weeks will eliminate this pest. Continue treatment until no gnats are seen flying. Avoid getting Sevin dust on the leaves as leaf burn can occur."

Sunburn often appears on the stems of plumerias when rooted cuttings have been transplanted and moved into full sun after weeks or months in filtered light or light shade conditions. The result is a bit unsightly but we have never seen plants adversely affected. Leaves can also exhibit signs of scorching. There are a number of potential causes: watering in the heat of the day when water droplets can magnify the sun's rays; the combination of intense sun and air pollution (causing yellowing and dropping of leaves); watering with tap water containing excessive salts; fertilizing with products having a high salt index. It is interesting to note that plumerias will grow under very difficult seaside conditions and, though often showing salt and wind burn on the leaves, will continue to grow and bloom. With sufficient organic matter added to beach sand, we have seen them adapt to planting on the beach only 50 feet from the water.

Stem rot is usually due to an excess amount of moisture when rooting cuttings or to moisture combined with cold temperatures during winter storage. It may also be due to overwatering or poor soil that retains too much moisture. Careful watering and close attention to the moisture holding capacity of the growing medium are the best ways to avoid the problem. Once stem rot begins it moves very quickly. If you cut back to solid material (no brown showing) you can often save the remaining portion of the plant. It is a good idea to dust this with dusting sulphur or a fungicide.

Although we have attempted be be as thorough as possible in defining the potential problems and solutions concerning plumeria pests and diseases, we stress once again that plumerias are exceptionally resistant to both. By maintaining healthy plants, observing them carefully and treating potential problems in the early stages, one will find that plumerias are among the world's toughest and most resistant species, rewarding us with untold wealth and beauty with a minimum of care.

DORMANCY

All the plumeria species and cultivars we have studied, with the exception of *P. obtusa* and some of its varieties and cultivars, have a dormant period (1 to 3 months, according to climate zones) in which they cease growth and flowering, usually shedding their leaves, as they store energy for the next season. This dormancy extends from the onset of cooler weather in the late fall to the first warm days of spring when the plant will once again initiate growth.

Some variations in this cycle should be noted. Many seedlings will go through their first and often second years without shedding their leaves. One may even find that in a group of mature plants of about the same age and growing under the same cultural and climatic conditions, some will shed their leaves while others will hold them throughout the winter and continue growth again in the spring.

Climate is not necessarily a factor in either the retention or shedding of leaves. In the tropics, especially in areas such as South India, where the temperature on a "cold", windy night in January might plummet to 68 degrees farenheit, most plumerias still drop their leaves. Another interesting phenomena is that the evergreen species, *P. obtusa*, also sheds its leaves for a brief period every 2 or 3 years.

During dormancy, plumerias do not require water since they are not producing flowers or leaves. In fact, excessive watering in the dormant months of winter usually leads to stem rot. Occasionally a plumeria will initiate an inflorescence late in the season just before the onset of cold weather. We have observed that it will begin to elongate and then discontinue growth. Many times it will drop during the winter, but we have seen a number of them remain on dormant plants and flower in the spring.

Plants that are placed in a sunny window and allowed to continue growing during the winter should be watered sparingly, about the same as other tropical foliage houseplants during cold weather. Fertilizing should be discontinued during this time as uptake of nutrients is slowed considerably. Given proper culture, we have seen evergreen varieties in full bloom in the home in December!

As mentioned above, dormancy varies somewhat according to climate. Some of our trees at the Matrimandir Gardens were deciduous for no more than 2 weeks. Others dropped their leaves for about 6 weeks. In temperate and sub-tropical climates dormancy often extends to 3 or 4 months. In Hawaii, trees are deciduous from late December through February, and in California for about 4 months. An interesting note on mature trees; a friend in Pondicherry, South India, has studied plumerias for years and has noted that mature trees of *P. rubra forma acutifolia* (25 years and older) drop their leaves with the onset of the monsoon (late October and early November) for 6 to 8 weeks. A definitive study should be conducted on dormancy in plumerias and the effects of day-length and temperature fluctuations on species and cultivars.

COLD TOLERANCE

Although plumerias must be considered tropicals and cultivated as such, especially in temperate areas, there are encouraging signs of greater cold tolerance exhibited in some cultivars in southern California. Since plumerias are frequently planted in the ground in these areas, it would be a valuable study to determine which cultivars are the most cold tolerant. This information could extend the outdoor growing season in much of the southern U.S.

For now, thanks to our many correspondents, we have a few items of interest to report. From plumeria growers in California we are informed that *P. obtusa* ('Singapore') is the least cold tolerant of all and can only be grown successfully in the ground in the mildest coastal areas. Among cultivars that have shown somewhat greater cold tolerance are 'Plastic Pink' and 'Celadine'; among the most cold hardy are 'Candy Stripe', 'Dean Conklin', 'Kaneohe Sunburst', 'Mela Matson', 'Scott Pratt', and 'Samoan Fluff'. 'Irma Bryan' has also survived light frosts with only the growing tips showing damage.

An interesting note concerning cold tolerance comes from a friend in California who has planted plumerias as a large hedge around the border of her yard. She has observed that occasional freezes (28 to 30 degrees F.) lasting only an hour or two will turn the tips of her plants black. The tips then die back about 3 or 4 inches, she breaks off the blackened area, and in the spring the plants produce from 1 to 5 new growing tips just below the break.

We should note once again that discontinuing the use of fertilizer in late summer will enable plants to harden off and reduce the susceptibility of tender growth to freeze damage. There is some evidence that applications of potassium during the growing season tend to build starch reserves in the trunks and limbs of trees and contribute to greater cold tolerance, but we have no confirmed data on this regarding plumerias. It has been noted, however, that plumerias will develop greater cold hardiness with age.

OVERWINTERING

Two major problems concerning winter protection for tropical plants are well known. The first is finding a place for them and the second is getting them into place! Plumerias are an additional challenge, especially older plants that have gained considerable height and spread. The problem of winter storage is also compounded for many plumeria afficionados who may have as many as 50 or 60 plants. (We know a few who have to find a place to store hundreds!)

Plumeria growers have long followed the standard practice of bringing plants into greenhouses and keeping the temperature as high as economically feasible, or into the house and trying to solve the logistics nightmare of finding enough sunny windows.

In the early 1980's, the late Frank Tuxworth and a few intrepid plumeria growers in Houston (where a light freeze or two each year is seemingly inevitable, and occasionally a "Blue Norther" will send temperatures into the teens), decided to experiment with overwintering techniques. These courageous and innovative individuals removed their plants from the containers, carefully shaking the soil off the roots, wrapped them in burlap or newspaper, and stored them in a closet, spare bedroom or warm attic. In the spring they brought their plants out after danger of frost was past, repotted them in fresh, well-drained, fertile soil and watched them burst into leaf and bloom!

The technique they discovered is entirely safe since plumerias have a marked dormancy. Plants that are left in their pots need no water at all while they are in storage as long as the plant is well established and has a good root system. It seems to matter little whether some or all of the soil is removed, whether plants are kept in darkness or receive a little light, whether the leaves are removed or left on (they'll drop off anyway), or what is used to wrap them, as long as they are kept above 40 degrees F.

During the past few years we have experimented with storing plants of all sizes and have found that perfectly healthy and well-rooted cuttings — but ones that had not rooted until late in the summer in community pots — tended to develop stem rot which often travels through the entire container. For this reason we recommend that they be transplanted into individual pots and kept growing during the first winter. Watering can be cut back considerably but not withheld altogether.

If you have many plants to store and not much space, we would suggest the following as the safest procedure to use:

Wait until the temperature starts dropping into the upper 40's. Allow plants to dry thoroughly before removing them from their containers and shake off enough soil to facilitate handling and transporting. Cover the roots with newspaper or wrapping paper and secure with twine. If you remove the leaves the plants will pack more tightly and you avoid having to clean up dead leaves in the spring. (It is best to remove the leaves a day or so before packing so the latex will dry thoroughly.) Store where temperatures will remain well above freezing and bring plants out again in the spring when nighttime temperatures are no longer dropping below 40 degrees F.. Do not be concerned if plants show some dessication or shriveling of their branches; they will rapidly fill out once watering and growth is resumed.

Even though it sounds drastic, the success rate with this technique of overwintering has been phenomenal. The only drawback we have noticed with the soilless storage method is that flowering tends to be somewhat delayed in the spring. If you have only a few plants, we recommend keeping them in their containers, but following the other proceedures outlined above. Both ways are not only convenient and practical but enable us to increase our collection of plumerias and therefore our enjoyment of more numerous colors and forms.

Removing Plants from the Ground for Winter Storage

In warmer sections of the U.S. there are a number of advantages to planting directly in the ground as discussed in the chapter on Planting and Transplanting. Removing plants from the ground is not a very difficult task. The mass of plumeria roots is rather modest compared to the amount of top growth plants can develop in a season. We have successfully transplanted fully grown trees more than 12 feet in height and 15 feet across and have never lost one. The following directions may be used as a general guide to transplanting most plants:

1. Dig only when soil moisture is sufficient to hold a ball together.

2. Use a sharp spade (or sharpshooter) with straight sides.

3. Dig in a circle around the trunk — a 1 foot radius will give you a 2 foot ball which should be sufficient for all but extremely large trees.

4. Dig straight down all around the tree. Do not pry up.

5. Make a second line of cuts outside the first on an angle towards the trunk to meet the bottom of the first cuts. Then undercut as deeply as possible towards the trunk.

6. This should loosen the ball completely and preserve the maximum number of roots.

7. It is best to work with another person (husbands and wives take note!) to remove the ball from the hole as this is physically taxing work and 2 additional hands will also help keep the ball intact.

8. If you wish to keep some soil around the roots yet reduce the size of the ball, it is easy to shave it once you have it out of the ground.

9. If you would like to bare root your plant you can either wash the soil off with water, gently loosen it with fingers or cultivator, or shake steadily and firmly.

GROWING PLUMERIAS INDOORS AND UNDER LIGHTS

As mentioned in the beginning of our handbook, people as far north as Canada are flowering plumerias indoors. Give them a sunny location for enough hours of the day and plumerias will flower easily providing their other requirements such as watering and fertilizing are met.

For information on growing and flowering plumerias under lights we quote from letters by Jerry A. Neyman in Denver, Colorado, and George F. Slusser in Woodinville, Washington. George writes that his ". . . eight year old plumeria does not lose its leaves in winter when the temperature does not drop below 60 degrees F., either in a south window or under fluorescent lights. I kept this plant dry and under fluorescent lights and it appears to be more vigorous this spring by producing more leaves per length of the stem."

Jerry has written a very detailed account of his experiences in growing and flowering plumerias under fluorescent 'Grow Lights', valuable information that we are pleased to share. We would like to note that he also sent us a photo of one of his plumerias in full bloom under lights! Jerry achieved his initial flowering in March 1986, from an unnamed yellow. The plant was 12 inches high and planted in a 6 inch pot. In a 48 inch shop-light fixture he put two 40 w. GE 'Wide Spectrum' bulbs. He placed the plant in the center of the bulbs, at a distance of 8 inches and gave the plant 16½ hours of light, fertilizing with ¼ strength 15-30-15 every watering. Humidity was kept at 70% using a cool mist humidifier as the source. Temperature was kept at 75 to 78 degrees during the day and 60-65 degrees at night. In June 1986, Jerry wrote: ". . . one plumeria plant (above) is under fluorescent grow lights. Plant grows steadily, without any growth problems, leaves are medium to light green in color, 8-10 inches in length, and a crispy hardness. It has been my observation that this 'hardness' of leaves indicates favorable growing conditions, especially light requirements are a prerequisite for flowering."

In December 1987, Jerry placed a plant of 'Kimo' and another unnamed yellow under a new light source, a 2 foot x 4 foot five-bulb light fixture, using four 'Gro-Lux' and one 'Cool White' bulb. This time he kept the humidity a bit higher, 75 to 80%, and the day temperature from 80-82 degrees with night temperatures averaging 70 to 75 degrees. He also kept two 6-inch fans on either side of the room to provide air movement. Both plants were in small pots, 5 and 6 inches respectively. This time he fertilized with high phosphorous fertilizers, BR 61 and Super Bloom, at ¼ strength, alternating with each watering.

Again, we quote his most interesting conclusions: "It has been my observation that plumerias will grow much faster and initiate the flowering process under a higher light intensity. Light intensity is the key, the most important factor in the proper growth and flowering of plumerias under 'Gro-Lights'". (Note: This corresponds exactly with Dr. Criley's experience using the silver shield to increase light intensity.) Jerry continues: "With the correct light intensity, regular feedings and favorable growing conditions, it will take approximately 3½ to 4 mos. for initiation of flower bud set."

Within 4 months Jerry had both plants developing flower buds and all this took place in his basement!

Photograph courtesy Dr. Richard A. Criley

Mela Matson

Peachglow Shell

Espinda

Carmen

Hausten White

Grove Farm

Loretta

King Kalakaua

PLUMERIAS IN THE LANDSCAPE

DESIGNING WITH PLUMERIAS

One of our most memorable experiences of plumerias in the landscape occurred while visiting the Singapore Botanical Garden. We were walking along the rise of a small hill when suddenly below us were the tops of plumeria trees, a visual symphony of color and fragrance. This special moment prompted us to consider using plumerias in the design of the Matrimandir Gardens in this way, for the enchantment of looking down on a valley of plumeria flowers clustered on a living carpet of dense green foliage was unforgettable. Similarly, those in sub-tropical and tropical areas, could sweep up from dwarf and semi-dwarf varieties to intermediate and finally the tallest varieties. There are so many creative ways to use plumerias. They are the conversation piece of the neighborhood as front yard trees and one often sees them in full bloom throughout the summer. We plant them in half barrels as accent pieces or mass a number of containers together to create a palette of color in our landscape. Given enough hours of sunlight they can transform atriums and courtyards into tropical oases.

COMPANION PLANTS

During our years in the tropics we experimented with plants that would be compatible with the dominant and imposing form of plumerias. We found bougainvilleas to be excellent companion plants, especially as ground covers around our plumerias, for they were at peak bloom in India when plumerias were fully deciduous. We planted some of the more colorful bougainvilleas at the base of several plumerias where they could climb into the branches and festoon the trees with color when leafless in early spring.

Here in the U.S., where most people must grow their plants in containers, the challenge is a bit different. Ours is a tropical garden and we like to have as many plants in bloom as possible every day of the year. In September and October, when plumerias wind down from their months of spectacular display, there are dozens of varieties of gingers, also famed for the beauty of their blossoms, their many colors and sweet fragrances. In the spring we have flowering bulbs, early gingers (Curcumas, Kaempferias, etc.), the renaissance of dwarf bananas (if we haven't had a hard freeze they will continue growth and flowering throughout the year), and a succession of perennials and flowering vines from early spring until winter. All of these combine harmoniously with plumerias, the "centerpieces" of our tropical garden.

We change the color displays under our potted plumerias each year and enjoy a long season of color from the flowering annuals and perennials spilling over the half-barrels and pots. Our greatest success has been with such plants as verbena, especially *Verbena peruviana* in various shades of lavender and pink, trailing periwinkle in white, pink and lavender-pink, the blue evolvulus, and many colors of moss rose and purslane. These and other low-growing bedding plants add a colorful touch and fullness to the base of plumerias that delights the eye and soften the look of container planting.

Beautiful must be the mountains whence ye come,
And bright in the fruitful valleys the streams,
wherefrom
Ye learn your song:
Where are those starry woods? O might I wander there,
Among the flowers, which in that heavenly air
Bloom the year long!

Bridges,
Nightingales

Plumeria tree

10

INTERESTING ACCOUNTS
AND OBSERVATIONS

Plumerias are known for unusual habits that often go against the norm . . . .

We have a mature plant that produced an inflorescence, and instead of falling off, it began to produce vegetative growth on top, sprouting new leaves as if it were a branch!

At the Matrimandir gardens we named one plant 'Hexiad' because of its ability to consistently produce six-petalled flowers.

Since vegetative reproduction assures us that a new plant will be identical to the plant from which it was taken, how is it that a cutting of a red cultivar will bloom pink or yellow the next year? Although we have not experienced this phenomena, close friends and long time plumeria growers have seen it happen numerous times, and yes, our friends are of sound mind and body!

Some plants exhibit the most extraordinary growth habits. A perfectly healthy plant will refuse to grow upwards despite the same culture as all other plants surrounding it. We once named a plant 'Cascade' because it only grew downward and swept the ground with its graceful branches. Another we named, 'Pink Splash', because it normally produced pure white flowers but often added a splash of pink to one or more blossoms.

Some of our interesting stories are not solely about plumeria plants. Last year Bill and Marcella Harmon of Worthington, Ohio, wrote to us of the history behind the "Frangipani Room" in the Indiana Memorial Union at Indiana University. According to Marcella:

> The alma mater song for New Albany, Indiana High School has these
> words:

> > "Here's to her whose name we'll ever
> > Cherish in our songs.
> > Dear old high school, dear old high school,
> > Praise to her belongs.
> > Glorianna, Frangipanna, here's to her success.
> > We to her will eer be faithful
> > Hail N.A.H.S."

> For many years, I sang this song with emotion and lusty vigor. While in high school, I would sing it to help our teams fight the hated foe. . . .

Vaguely, I supposed that 'Glorianna Frangipanna' was Latin meaning something like 'glorious friendship'. Since I still bear the scars of Latin I and II, I never had the slightest inclination to pursue the research any farther. At our 50th high school class reunion, someone asked the question, "Why are the words 'Glorianna Frangipanna' in our school song? I have researched the words and nothing I have found makes sense."

I checked and he was right so I vowed to find the answer in time for our 55th reunion.

My first impulse was to hunt up some old guy and ask him. Then I realized that we are the old guys.

Finally, after many investigations, I found a reference librarian who said there is a Frangipani Room in the Student Union at the University of Indiana with a plaque explaining the name.

I wrote the IU Student Union and received the enclosed information. So the whole thing apparently started with a bunch of 'spirited' students hunting for rhyming words for 'Indiana'. Frangipana is certainly better than top banana or grand piano.

Whoever assumed the task of creating the alma mater for New Albany High School simply changed a few words to 'Hail to old IU' and presto— we have our Glorianna Frangipanna.

The song, according to its author, Joe T. Giles, A.B., '94 had its beginning on October 24, 1892 when some fifty students boarded the Monon to Lafayette for the Purdue football game. During the ride, someone mentioned the need for a new college yell. One with Indiana in it.

But what would rhyme with Indiana? Gloriana suggested one. Then into the mind of Ernest H. Lindley, A.B., '93 who often helped in his father's drugstore, flashed the name of a popular perfume of that day — Frangipana which was derived from Frangipani, a tropical tree or shrub of Mexico, Jamaica, the Guianas and elsewhere. Thus came the alliterative first line of the new yell — "Gloriana, Frangipana, Indiana".

Finally, this note from Marcella: "We are one of the newer members of your Plumeria family and I want to give you a status report. The class bought Plumeria seeds ... last fall as part of our 55th High School Class Reunion. The class member with the best Frangipani wins a prize at our 60th reunion." She writes further: "The Harmons have four lusty sprouts that have happily soaked up the winter sun in our south-facing bay window. Our contest entrant seems like it is off to a good start."

ADDITIONAL NOTES, QUOTES & ANECDOTES

***The Oxford English Dictionary offers the following definitions and interesting derivations for the name Frangipani.

Frangipane - (said to be from Frangipani, the name of the inventor.)

1. A perfume prepared from, or imitating the odour of, the flower of the red jasmine.

1676 Shadwell *Virtuoso* III H4A "I have choice of good Gloves, Amber, Orangery, Genoa Romaine, Frangipand" (sic.)

1727-1741 Chambers *Cycl.*, *Frangipane*, an exquisite kind of perfume.

2. The red jasmine tree (*Plumiera rubra*), from the flower of which the perfume is prepared. 1866 *Treas. Bot.*, Frangipane, *Plumiera rubra*.

3. In various applications: see quotes.

1844 Hoblyn *Med. Dict. Frangipan*, an extract of milk, for preparing artificial milk, made by evaporating skimmed milk to dryness, mixed with almonds and sugar.

1858 Simmonds *Dict. Trade*, Franchipane, Frangipane, a kind of pastry, a cake of cream, almonds, spice, etc.

attrib. 1892 Garrett *Encycl. Cookery*, *Frangipane Flawn. . . Frangipane paste.*

1895 Jusserand *Eng. Ess.* 98 Lafleur, whom he often asked to make frangipane tarts.

***Here's a recipe we found cut out of a magazine (author unknown but our appreciation nonetheless for the word frangipane - and the excellent recipe!)

Apricot Tart

Here is a simple-to-make recipe that really highlights the brief apricot season.

> To prepare apricots:
> 2 dozen apricots
> 1 1/2 cups sugar
> 2 cups water
> For the frangipane:
> 4 T. sugar
> 4 T. butter
> 1 egg plus 1 egg yolk
> 4 T. almonds, finely ground (use a food processor, blender or coffee grinder)
> 1 t. vanilla
> pinch of salt
> For the glaze:
> 3/4 cup apricot preserves
> 3 T. water
> For the pastry:
> 2 cups flour
> 1/4 cup sugar
> 3/4 cup butter, cut into bits
> 1 egg

Wash and pit apricots. In saucepan, bring sugar and water to boil, lower heat to simmer and add apricot halves. For the very ripe fruit simmer 30 seconds to 1 minute; moderately ripe fruit, 3 to 4 minutes.

Remove carefully with a slotted spoon and drain upside down on several thicknesses of paper toweling.

To make frangipane filling, cream butter and sugar until smooth. Add eggs and blend well. Add ground almonds, vanilla and salt and stir until smooth.

For pastry, sift together flour and sugar. Add butter and, using pastry blender, knives or fingertips, blend until mixture is in small crumbs. With a fork stir in egg and blend well. Work paste into a ball, wrap in plastic and refrigerate 30 minutes or more. Press chilled dough into a 10-inch tart pan with fingertips, about 1/4-inch thick all around.

Spread frangipane over bottom of crust with a spoon. Arrange apricot halves on top, overlapping them slightly. Bake in 400-degree oven 50-55 minutes, until frangipane is set.

Heat preserves with water in a small saucepan until hot, stirring to prevent burning. Spoon evenly over apricots while tart is still hot.

***From the opposite side of the world, — and a long way from the subject of Apricot tarts, — we learn that in Thailand plumerias are never planted around the home but are common around temples and in cemeteries. The Thai name, (transliterated into Roman letters), is "lun tom", meaning "sadness". Unlike many other tropical areas where frangipani flowers are worn in women's hair or made into fragrant leis, in Thailand it is only recently becoming popular to wear them and then only on New Year's Day!

***As new and exotic plants are introduced to American gardens, the leading horticultural magazines often publish articles on their culture. During the past nine years we have seen a number of articles on plumerias featured in the following publications.

Sunset Magazine - Aug. 1986 "Hawaii's Lei Flower" Sunset staff

Flower & Garden - Dec. 1988 - "The Fragrant Plumerias" by Richard M. Eggenberger

American Horticulturist - Apr. 1991 "The Moragne Plumerias" by Richard A. Criley and Jim Little

HousePlant Magazine Fall 1993 "A Passion For Plumerias" by William C. Mulligan

HousePlant Magazine Spring 1994 "Plumerias: A Tropical Treat" by Richard and Mary Helen Eggenberger

Sunset Garden Guide Spring-Summer 1994 "Tropical Delights" by Michael MacCaskey

11

RESEARCH ON PLUMERIAS

Studies on Branching

A study on branching has been conducted under the direction of Dr. Richard Criley at the University of Hawaii. Dr. Criley has written us recently that the project will not be completed for several months more but so far it has been found that ". . . lanolin paste applications of N-6-benzyladenine (rates from 0.5 to 4 mg BA per gram of lanolin) to cut stumps/branches produced an increased number of breaks over the controls, but there were insufficient replications for good statistics."

In 1973 Dr.Criley published some valuable research in the <u>Horticulture Digest</u>, a publication of the Cooperative Extension Service, University of Hawaii, entitled "Investigations into Plumeria Flowering". He has kindly allowed me to include this research in our handbook. We quote in full:

Investigations into Plumeria Flowering

by Richard A. Criley, Associate Horticulturist

Based on work on other flower crops showing regrowth and flowering following cut-back, we attempted to time plumeria ('Common Yellow') for winter flowering by cutting back during summer. Ten plants were cut back to leave 8- to 12-inch stubs on July 1, July 22, and August 15. Half of each treatment was placed in front of silver-painted boards to provide more total light.

Regrowth was longest on the earliest cut-back, but no treatment showed early flower bud development, nor did the reflector appear to influence earlier flowering.

That year, however, on 72 breaks developing on the 15 plants in front of the reflector, there were 21 inflorescences while on 70 breaks on the other group, only 15 inflorescences developed. During the next year, the plants in front of the reflector produced 29 inflorescences on the original breaks plus 12 more on the shoots produced below some of the 21 inflorescences of the year before, for a total of 41 inflorescences. The plants without the reflector had 19 inflorescences and none on breaks which subtended the previous year's inflorescences.

The reflector apparently was responsible for doubling the number of inflorescences produced in two seasons following a severe cut-back. The actual amount of light could not be accurately measured but it was estimated that there was about 33 percent reflectance.

Another research project Dr. Criley has shared with us is entitled "Flowering of Young Plumeria Cuttings". Since the research is too lengthy to quote in full we will abstract some of the most important data:

An alternative to outdoor flower production of plumerias during winter is to force the inflorescences of budded shoots in a heated greenhouse. The advantages would be more dense spacing, ease of harvest, and ability to harvest every flower produced. We do not know if the inflorescence can be induced to develop if the shoot is removed from the rest of the plant and not allowed to form roots, but it is possible to root these shoots as cuttings and force the inflorescence. In addition to the implications for winter production of plumeria flowers for leis, such a system would be happily embraced by producers of cuttings for sale to Hawaii's tourists.

This is a report on a preliminary study which demonstrates the concept of forcing rooted cuttings into bloom when a bud is already present in the terminal.

The following is a brief summary of the experiment: cuttings were rooted in one gallon pots in the fall of 1973. Rooted plants showing buds were then forced in a warm greenhouse in December. A teaspoon of Osmokote 14-14-14 was topdressed on each pot and irrigation was by hand, as needed. Greenhouse temperatures fluctuated between 64 and 93 degrees F. (N/D), averaging 74 to 79 degrees F. Although the inflorescence size was smaller for the forced plants in containers than for field-grown plants, one group averaged 104 flowers per inflorescence, while the duration of flowering averaged from 5 weeks to 12 weeks for the same variety. During the peak of flowering at the 3rd and 4th weeks, the same cultivar produced an average of 16 flowers per plant per week. This should be a great encouragement to anyone who would like to grow plumerias under greenhouse conditions during the winter months.

For those who would like to experiment further, we quote the final paragraph of Dr. Criley's paper:

The results of this trial lend some optimism to the concept of developing a system for production of plumeria flowers during winter months, but many questions remain to be investigated. While we have demonstrated the ability to force flowers on rooted shoots of plumerias during the winter, this does not necessarily mean that budded, but unrooted, shoots would respond similarly although we have observed flower development to anthesis on branches which have been left lying in the field after pruning. A means to identify shoots in which the inflorescence has been initiated must be found so that a high proportion of productive plants can be assembled for winter forcing. While the temperatures encountered during this experimental period were sufficient to permit forcing, we do not know how cool temperatures would have to be to delay development. We would also like to know what must be done in order for an inflorescence to produce up to the potential observed on field-grown plants.

During the 1970's some research was conducted in India on the structure of cymes and a new hybrid named in honor of former prime minister Indira Gandhi was introduced.

In the May 1980 issue of The Planter, published in Kuala Lumpur, Malaysia, there is an article on the viablility of plumeria seeds (Mossel in Amsterdam successfully germinated seeds 16 months old), percentage of germination and studies on the insertion of cotyledons.

There have been several highly technical studies listed in the Horticultural Abstracts which we researched from 1968 through 1988, some concerning the reversion of embryos in Plumeria rubra, others detailing the finding of iridoids with algicidal properties in the roots of plumerias, an in-depth study of chromosome counts that should be of much importance in future breeding, and one study on the fragrance of one species of plumeria. Other than the studies quoted above and the important observations of dedicated plumeria growers, there is not much more to be found.

Locally, some important work has been accomplished by Elizabeth Thornton. In one experiment she sprayed gibberellic acid on new flower buds when they were just ⅛ to ¼ inch high and found that this treatment increased seed set. She has also researched Nature's pollinators, and has related her observations on the hummingbird, the hummingbird hawk moth and the braconid in her 1985 revision of The Exotic Plumeria.

George Slusser of Woodinville, Washington, continues to send us detailed accounts of his experiments in germination and rooting plumeria cuttings in water, a fascinating study, which we have included in the chapter on Propagation.

Michael Pettit of Garland, Texas, is working on closed pollination in an attempt to develop hybrids that will flower easily in temperate climates and will be more compact.

Dr. Criley has recently sent me two progress reports on further research on plumerias undertaken through grants from the Plumeria Society of America. The first study is to determine the effect of growth retardants on stem elongation of P. 'Common Yellow'. Preliminary research indicates that all four of the retardants used seem to be effective, with marked effects at higher concentrations. The second study is on the effect of growth regulators on branching of P. 'Common Yellow'. A third study concerns the storage longevity of plumeria flowers and ethylene production by plumeria flowers. The best temperature to hold flowers was determined to be 10 degrees C. The longest lasting cultivars were 'Irma Bryan', 'Elena', 'Common Yellow', 'White Shell', 'Pauahi Alii' (formerly 'Angus Gold') and 'Peachglow Shell'. We quote from the final few sentences of Dr. Criley's preliminary report:

Addition of ethylene to the holding environment did hasten the development of browning when compared to an ethylene-free system or a system to which air was flushed to remove accumulated ethylene.

The implication of this work is that ethylene is probably involved in reducing the keeping life of harvested (and old) plumeria flowers. If some way can be found to prevent the action of ethylene, it may be possible to extend the keeping life of plumerias used in leis or as cut flowers.

It is most gratifying to us to be able to receive reports from all parts of the world relating to current studies on plumerias and to share this information with interested plumeria growers. In this way we all benefit by a greater understanding of Nature's extraordinary gifts. As the poet and sage, Sri Aurobindo, has written: "All's miracle here and can by miracle change."

PLUMERIA SOURCES

Although many local nurseries now offer plumerias and other tropicals such as mandevilla, the best mail order source is:

Stokes Tropicals
P.O. Box 9868
New Iberia, LA 70562-9868
1-800-624-9706
email: gstokes@1stnet.com

Glenn and Yvonne Stokes offer an extraordinary selection of plumerias and other colorful tropicals and semi-tropicals such as hibiscus, bougainvilleas, gingers, bananas, heliconias, and bromeliads. They also have an excellent website with great color photos of the plants they offer: www.stokestropicals.com

12

ORGANIZATIONS AND SOURCES

Undoubtedly the finest plumeria research station is the University of Hawaii's Waimanolo Research Station on Oahu, under the direction of Dr. Richard A. Criley.

Some of the major collections of the world may be found at the Matrimandir Gardens, Auroville, South India; the Singapore Botanic Gardens; Koko Head Crater near Diamond Head on Oahu (devoted exclusively to plumerias); the Calcutta Botanic Gardens; Foster Botanical Gardens in Honolulu; the Botanic Gardens on the island of St. Vincent; and the Waimea Arboretum in Haleiwa, on Oahu's North Shore.

THE HISTORY OF THE PLUMERIA SOCIETY

The Plumeria Society of America, Inc. was incorporated in 1979 as a non-profit organization devoted exclusively to research, education, and registration of plumerias. The Society was founded by three dedicated women, Nancy Ames, Nadine Barr, and Elizabeth Thornton, with the aim of furthering the knowledge of all aspects of plumeria cultivation in non-tropical climates. They also wished to convey their love and experience with these magnificent exotic plants that could be grown in containers in all areas of the U.S. and in the ground in the warmest areas of the South and West.

The propagation, culture, classification, identification of species and registration of plumeria cultivars are only a few of the areas in which The Plumeria Society educates and encourages its members to participate. During the past fifteen years the Society has sponsored numerous flower shows, organized visits to members' gardens to study plumeria collections, arranged tours to Hawaii to observe plumerias in a tropical habitat, and held yearly conferences with seminars given by experts in various fields. The Society awards grants for research on plumerias and has funded projects through the University of Hawaii, University of Houston, and Texas A&M University.

The Plumeria Society of America offers both regular and associate memberships and publishes a newsletter, "Plumeria Potpourri", which keeps members and associate members informed of the latest developments.

Further information may be obtained by writing to:

The Plumeria Society of America, Inc.
P.O. Box 22791
Houston, TX 77227-2791

The Southern California Plumeria Society was founded by Mr. Henry M. Dupree in 1999. Mr. Dupree serves as President with Mr. Carl Herzog as Vice-President. The society began with 25 members and now numbers almost 100. They meet the last Sunday of the month in Balboa Park, San Diego, and currently have flower shows twice a year.

INDEX OF ILLUSTRATIONS AND COLOR PHOTOGRAPHS

APPENDIX A

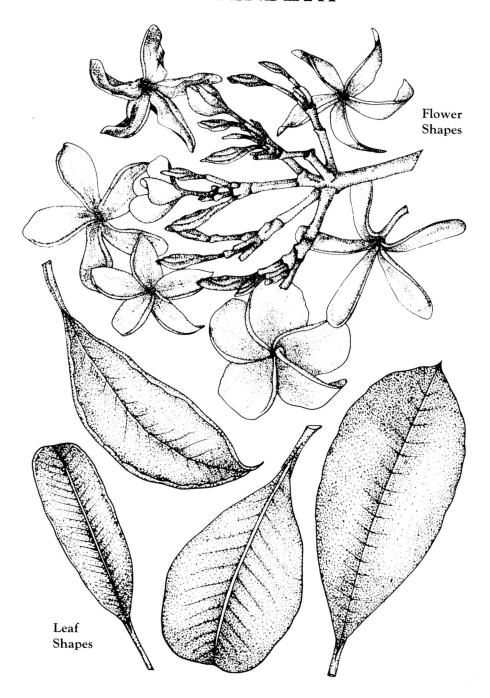

Flower
Shapes

Leaf
Shapes

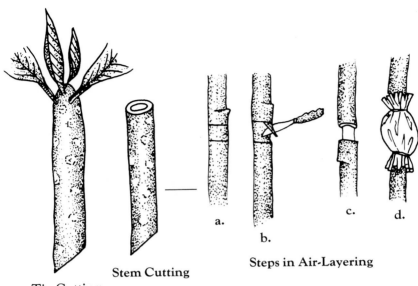

Tip Cutting

Stem Cutting

Steps in Air-Layering

a.

b.

c.

d.

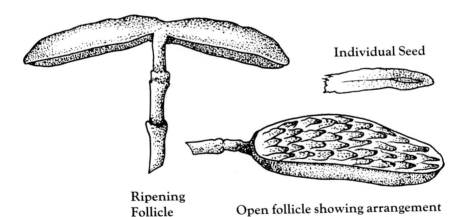

Individual Seed

Ripening
Follicle

Open follicle showing arrangement
of seeds on one side.

Reproductive Parts of a Plumeria

Mary Helen standing by a mature 'Dwarf Deciduous', against a dramatic backdrop of an approaching storm in the mountains.

Petite Pink — The car in the background shows the scale of this mature, exceptionally dwarf plumeria grown for many years in good soil.

These two unnamed hybrids of considerable beauty were photographed in Hawaii. New plumeria cultivars are discovered every year in all parts of the world from seedlings of unknown parentage.

Bali Whirl — The world's first double flowered plumeria with ten petals.

Photo courtesy Glenn M. Stokes

Caroline B™ — A very special new seedling of Pink Pansy. 4″ white flower with a strong pink edge and a gold and pink center with pink rays radiating from the center. Good frangipani fragrance.

Princess Victoria™ — The first variegated flower available to the public. A seedling from Metairie Pink. Large (3-3 1/2″) spectacular red and white splotched flowers with butter yellow centers. Good gardenia fragrance. Keeping quality good.

Plumeria pudica

Photo courtesy Emerson Willis

Lemon Drop — Many collectors consider this hard-working tree one of the premier yellows. It is an easy to root, multi-branching, symmetrical cultivar adorned with huge clusters of 3 3/4″ bright lei-quality flowers possessing an unusual citrus scent that is quite strong.

Guillot's Sunset — The flowers are multicolored, though primarily pink. The center of the flower is orange with a distinct line of red in the center of each petal. Petals are overlapping large ovals, and the texture is medium to heavy with a mild rose fragrance.

Photo courtesy Harry Leuzinger

San Germain — One of the most outstanding plumerias from Hawaii. Large white flowers (4′′-41/2′′) with hint of pink and large yellow centers. Good sweet fragrance. Heavy texture.

Photo courtesy Glenn M. Stokes

Moragne #93 (aka 'Reddish Moragne') — Recently Dr. Criley with the University of Hawaii and Jim Little renamed P. Reddish Moragne to P. Moragne #93. The flowers of this lovely cultivar are reddish pink with a yellow throat. The fragrance is sweet. Like most of the Moragne hybrids, the backs of the petals have a red band.

Photo courtesy Harry Leuzinger

Photo courtesy Harry Leuzinger

Kauanani — In the late 1980's, Jim Little and Dr. Richard Criley got a call from Gloria Schmidt who had some plumerias she had started from seed. The mature trees were going to be bulldozed during a property expansion, and Mrs. Schmidt wanted the cultivars saved. Dr. Criley took several cuttings back to the university where he grew them. One of the saved varieties was later named P. Kauanani, and it is a beautiful rich deep gold. Towards the edges of the petal, the reds and yellows mix in such a way that there appears to be a reddish glow. The plant has a wonderful upright growth habit, and the wood is of medium thickness. The flowers are produced abundantly and their texture is thick.

Photo courtesy Glenn M. Stokes

Sondra B™ — A new, very distinctinve seedling with large rounded overlapping pale pink petals with deeper shading on one side and deep rose pink bands on reverse. Yellow seems to bleed from the center. The 3-3 1/2″ flower has good tex-texture and a strong gardenia fragrance. Named for Glenn Stokes' daughter.

Abigail™ — A great new seedling from Maui Beauty. A white flower suffused with pink and a dark-yellow center. Petals are short and barely pointed. Reverse side of petals is a uniform deep pink. Flowers are 2 1/2″ across. A nice sweet fragrance: compact grower.

Photo courtesy Glenn M. Stokes

Bali Palace — A magnificent plumeria with rich golden yellow on both sides of the heavily textured petals. It has a moderately sweet fragrance and averages 2″ across. Flowers occur in large pendulous clusters. Discovered by Jim Little in King Gunadhi's Palace garden in Bali, Indonesia.

Photo courtesy Glenn M. Stokes

Gloria Schmidt — A lovely medium-size rainbow flower that combines the characteristics of Intense Rainbow, Lei Rainbow and Candy Stripe. Discovered by Dr. Richard Criley of the University of Hawaii.

Photo courtesy Glenn M. Stokes

Ryann Chelsey — This thick-branched tree produces huge clusters of 4″ pink blooms, heavily veined with a darker shade of pink. The orangey-yellow center has a faint corona of light ochre. The keeping quality is very good and the spicy scent is powerful. This cultivar has leaves up to 27″ long and 6″ wide. The Ryann Chelsey was registered by the Plumeria Society, Inc. in 1998 and named in honor of Emerson and Nancy Willis' granddaughter.

Emerson and Nancy Willis —
"Nan and the Plumeria Man"

GLOSSARY

Acuminate. Tapering with somewhat concave sides to a protracted, acute point.

Aestivation. The arrangement of the perianth or its parts in the bud.

Anther. The pollen-bearing part of the stamen.

Callus. In cuttings or on injuries, the thick new tissue that develops and covers the injury.

Cambium. A layer of formative cells between the wood and bark in woody plants: the cells increase by division and differentiate to form new wood and bark.

Cochleate. Coiled like a snail shell.

Comose. Bearing a tuft of soft hairs.

Corolla. The inner circle or second whorl of floral envelopes. (The outer whorl is the calyx.)

Cultivar. A horticultural variety or race that has originated and persisted under cultivation, not necessarily referable to a botanical species, and of botanical or horticultural importance, requiring a name.

Elliptical. Having the form of an ellipse as in certain leaves.

Endosperm. The starch and oil-containing tissue of many seeds; often referred to as the albumen.

Cotyledon. A seed leaf, a primary leaf in the embryo. Source of initial plant sustenance.

Follicle. A dry, dehiscent, one-carpelled fruit with usually more than one seed and opening only along the ventral suture. (In plumerias these resemble two downward-curving horns.)

Gamopetalus. With petals united to one another marginally, at least basally.

Genus. A more or less closely related and definable group of plants, including one or more species; the name of the genus becomes the first word of the binomial employed in horticultural and botanical literature. Thus, the oaks belong to the genus *Quercus*, the white oak is *Quercus alba*, etc.

Glabrous. Without hairs of any kind, not pubescent.

Inflorescence. 1) The mode of arrangement of the flowers on a plant; 2) the flowering part of a plant; 3) the coming into flower of a plant.

Lanceolate. Lance-shaped, several times longer than broad and widest below the middle, tapering with convex sides upward to the apex.

Membranaceous. Thin, soft and translucent, like a membrane.

Morphological. The characteristics of form and structure in plants.

Obovate. Inversely ovate, broader above rather than below the middle.

Obtuse. Blunt, rounded.

Pandurate. Fiddle-shaped, rounded at both ends and somewhat contracted at or about the middle.

Perianth. A collective term for the floral envelopes, the calyx, corolla or both.

Petiole. The stalk of a leaf.

Pistil. A unit of the gynoecium, composed of ovary, style (when present), and stigma.

Pubescent. Strictly, this means covered with soft, short, fine hairs; as commonly used, however, the term means hairy, bearing hairs in a generalized sense without reference to the type of hair.

Salverform. Said of a gamopetalus corolla with a slender tube and an abruptly expanded flat limb.

Sessile. Immediately attached by the base.

Stamen. The pollen-bearing organ of a seed plant.

Stigma. The apical part of the pistil, which receives the pollen grains and provides conditions necessary for their germination.

Style. The more or less elongated part of the pistil between the ovary and the stigma.

Subsessile. Not truly sessile; almost sessile.

Systematist. A taxonomist; a person who works according to a system.

Thrysiform. Shaped like a thyrse, thyrsus. A dense, panicle-like inflorescence in which the main axis is indeterminate and the lateral axes are determinate.

Undulate. Having a wavy edge.

Whorl. A circle of three or more leaves, flowers, or other organs at one node.

BIBLIOGRAPHY

Annals of the Missouri Botanical Garden — Volume XXV, 1938 -ref: Studies in the Apocynaceae VIII — Robert E. Woodson, Jr.

Badianus Manuscript, (in Latin), Francisco de Mendoza, Mexico D.F. 1552

Botany of the Maya Area-Miscellaneous Papers XIV — XXI, Publication 522, Carnegie Institution of Washington, Washington, D.C. 1940

Catologo Alfabetico de Nobres Vulgares y Cientificos de Plantas que Existen en Mexico — A.L. Herrera, Estudios Biologicos, Mexico 1923

Color in the Sky — Edwin A. Menninger, Horticultural Books, Inc. New York, 1975

Use Plumerias for Variety and Fragrance — Richard A. Criley, The Sunday Star Bulletin & Advertiser, Honolulu, Hawaii June 1981

Dictionary of the Economic Products of India, A — George Watt, Cosmo Pulblishers, Delhi 1896

Dictionary of Gardening — The Royal Horticultural Society, Edited by Fred J. Chittenden, Oxford at the Clarendon Press, 1951

Exotic Plumeria, The — Elizabeth H. Thornton with Sharon H. Thornton, Plumeria Specialties, Houston, Texas 1985

Exotica — A.B. Graf, 9th Ed. Roehrs Co. East Rutherford, New Jersey 1976

Familiar Flowering Trees in India, Ida Colthurst, Thacker, Spink & Co., Calcutta, India 1924

Flora of Baja California — Ira L. Wiggins, University Press, Stanford, California 1980

Flower Leis of Hawaii, The — Dorothy and Bob Hargreaves, Hargreaves Company Inc. Kailua, Hawaii 1971

Flowering Trees — M.S. Randhawa, National Book Trust, New Delhi, India, 1965

Flowering Trees and Shrubs in India — D.V. Cowen, Thacker, Spink & Co., Bombay, India 1969

Flowering Trees in Subtropical Gardens — Gunther Kunkel, Dr. W. Junk b.v. Publishers, The Hague — Boston — London 1978

Flowering Trees of the Caribbean — Introduction by William C. White, Illus. by Bernard and Harriet Pertchik, Rinehart & Company, New York 1951

Flowering Trees of the World — Edwin A. Menninger, Hearthside Press, Inc., New York 1962

Flowers and Their Messages — The Mother, Sri Aurobindo Ashram, Pondicherry, India 1979

Flowers of Guatemala — Carol Rogers Chickering, University of Oklahoma Press, Norman, OK 1973

Flowers of the World — Frances Perry, Hamlyn Publishers, London, 1972

Frangipani from Hawaii — Donald P. Watson, The Indian Journal of Horticulture — Pub. Dr. K.L. Chadha for the Horticultural Society of India — Kapoor Art Pres, New Delhi, June 1971

Hawaii Blossoms — Dorothy and Bob Hargreaves, Hargreaves Company, Inc., Kailua, Hawaii 1958

Hawaiian Flowers & Flowering Trees — Loraine E. Kuck & Richard C. Tongg, Charles E. Tuttle Company, Inc., Rutland, Vermont and Tokyo, Japan 1958

Hawaiian Plumerias — Watson, Chinn, Clay and Brewbaker, Circular 410, University of Hawaii Cooperative Extension Service, Honolulu, Hawaii 1965

Hortus Third — Staff of the L.H. Bailey Hortorium, Cornell University, Macmillan Publishing Company, New York, 1976

Index Kewensis — An Enumeration of the Genera and Species of Flowering Plants — Tomus II — Hooker and Jackson — Oxford, at the Clarendon Press MDCCCXCV — and supplements I, III, IV, V, VI, VII, VIII, IX, X, 1886-1940

In Gardens of Hawaii — Marie C. Neal, Bishop Museum Press, Honolulu, Hawaii 1965

Indian Trees — Dietrich Brandis, Periodical Experts Book Agency, Dehradun, India — reprint 1978, First Published 1906

Integrated System of Classification of Flowering Plants, An — Arthur Cronquist, The New York Botanical Gardens, Columbia University Press, New York 1981

Investigations into Plumeria Flowering — Richard A. Criley, Horticulture Digest, University of Hawaii, Cooperative Extension Service, December 1973

Life In Mexico — The Letters of Fanny Calderon de la Barca, Doubleday & Company, Inc. New York 1966

Manual of Gardening for India, 7th edition, revised — Firminger, W. Burns, Thacker, Spink & Co., Calcutta, India 1930

Martinique Revisited — Clarissa Therese Kimber, Texas A & M University Press, College Station, Texas 1988

Meet Flora Mexicana — M. Walter Pesman, Dale S. King, Publisher, Six Shooter Canyon, Globe, Arizona 1962

Mexican Flowering Trees and Plants — Helen O'Gorman, Edited by Ella Wallace Turok, Ammex Associados, Mexico City 1961

Mexican Plants for American Gardens — Cecile Hulse Matschat, Houghton Mifflin Co., New York 1935

Modern Tropical Garden, The — Loraine E. Kuck and Richard C. Tongg, Tongg Publishing Company, Honolulu, Hawaii 1960

New Illustrated Encyclopedia of Gardening — T.H. Everett, Greystone Press, New York 1960

New York Botanical Garden Illustrated Encyclopedia of Horticulture — Ed. T.H. Everett, Garland Publishing Co., New York 1984

100 Beautiful Trees of India — Charles McCann, Taraporevala Sons & Co. Bombay, India 1966

Ornamental Trees of Hawaii, The — Joseph F. Rock — Published under patronage — Honolulu, Hawaii 1917

Philippine Oranamental Plants and Their Care — Mona Lisa Steiner, Ph.D., Carmelo & Bauermann, Inc. Manila, Philippines 1960

Plantas Utiles de la Flora Mexicana — Maximino Martinez, Ediciones Botas, Mexico, D.F., 1959

Plumeria — Bulletin No.14 — National Botanic Gardens, Lucknow, India 1958

Plumeria Cultivars in Hawaii — James T. Chinn and Richard A. Criley, Research Bulletin 158, Hawaii Agricultural Experiment Station, College of Tropical Agriculture and Human Resources, University of Hawaii, Honolulu, Hawaii 1982

Secret Life of Plants, The — Peter Tompkins and Christopher Bird, Avon Books, New York 1973

Shrubs, Trees and Climbers — Sima Eliovson, Dai Nippon Printing Co., Hong Kong 1975

Some Beautiful Indian Trees — E. Blatter and Walter S. Millard, Natural History Society, Bombay, India 1954

Some observations on seeds and seedlings of frangipani (Plumeria L., Apocynaceae) — M. Ratnasabapathy and J. Mossel — The Planter, Vol 56 No. 650, United Selangor Press, Kuala Lumpur, Malaysia, May 1980

Some Madras Trees — A. Butterworth (Publisher and date missing)

Standard Cyclopedia of Horticulture — L.H. Bailey, The Macmillan Company, New York 1928

Studies in the Apocynaceae — Plumeria — Vol 25 — Woodson, Annals of the Missouri Botanical Garden, 1938

Sunset Magazine — August 1986 — Lane Publishing Co., Los Angeles, CA.

Taylor's Encyclopedia of Gardening — Edited by Norman Taylor — Fourth Edition, Houghton Mifflin Company, Boston 1961

Trees and Shrubs of Mexico — Paul C. Standley, Contributions from the United States National Herbarium, Volume 23, Part 4, Smithsonian Institution, Government Printing Office, Washington, D.C., 1924

Tropica — A.B. Graf, 3rd Edition, Roehrs Company, East Rutherford, New Jersey 1986

Tropical Gardening — T.M. Greensill, Frederick A. Praeger Pub., New York, Washington 1964

Tropical Gardening — Peggy Hickok Hodge, Tuttle & Co., Japan, 1975

Tropical Planting and Gardening — Nixon Smiley, University of Miami Press, Coral Gables, Florida 1960

Vegetation of Peten, The , Cyrus Longworth Lundell, Carnegie Institution of Washington, Washington, D.C. 1937

Wayside Trees of Malaya — E.J.H. Corner, Government Printing Office, Singapore — Second Edition 1952

Wild Flowers of the World — Text by Brian C. Morley, Crescent Books, New York

Wyman's Gardening Encyclopedia — Donald Wyman, MacMillan Publishing Co., New York 1977